Four-Legged Miracles

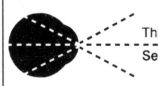

This Large Print Book carries the
Seal of Approval of N.A.V.H.

FOUR-LEGGED MIRACLES

HEARTWARMING TALES OF
LOST DOGS' JOURNEYS HOME

BRAD STEIGER AND
SHERRY HANSEN STEIGER

THORNDIKE PRESS
A part of Gale, Cengage Learning

Detroit • New York • San Francisco • New Haven, Conn • Waterville, Maine • London

GALE
CENGAGE Learning®

Library of Congress CIP DATA on file. Cataloguing in publication for this book
is available from the Library of Congress
ISBN-13: 978-1-4104-5791-2 (hardcover)
ISBN-10: 1-4104-5791-5 (hardcover)

Published in 2013 by arrangement with St. Martin's Press, LLC

Printed in the United States of America
1 2 3 4 5 6 7 17 16 15 14 13

CONTENTS

5

ACKNOWLEDGMENTS

We would like to thank those individuals who contributed their own experiences with "Four-Legged Miracles" who came home to them after going missing and causing a great deal of heartbreak in their absence. We are appreciative of the enthusiasm and the thoughtful guidance of our delightful editor, Michelle Richter, and we are grateful for the continued support and friendship of Agnes Birnbaum, our tireless and wonderful agent of many years. We must also acknowledge the unconditional love of our beloved Hans, our four-legged family member, and all those canine teachers who throughout our lives have shared our Earthwalk and who will live forever in cherished memories. Finally, we would like to recognize all those men and women who devote their lives to caring for and sheltering lost, abandoned, or abused dogs with the mis-

sion of returning or connecting them to loving families.

He is your friend, your partner, your defender, your dog. You are his life, his love, his leader. He will be yours, faithful and true, to the last beat of his heart. You owe it to him to be worthy of such devotion.

— UNKNOWN

Dogs are not our whole life, but they make our lives whole.

— ROGER CARAS

INTRODUCTION:
WE LOVE DOGS — AND GRIEVE
WHEN THEY GO MISSING

We love dogs, and it seems apparent that they love us. Some experts say that the spark of this love affair began as many as 140,000 years ago and that it has only become more intense as the centuries have moved onward. We love dogs so much that there are an estimated 500 million domesticated dogs in the world.

France has one of the highest dog-to-human ratios, with approximately seventeen dogs to every one hundred people in the nation. An unofficial census estimates over 10 million pooches in France, with over five hundred thousand in Paris alone. Over 40 percent of French dog owners state that their Fido or Fifi is the single most important thing in their lives, even more important than their lover. Lavishing expensive clothing, elegant restaurants, and exclusive spas on their dogs, the French spend an estimated three billion Euros on *les bons chiens* each year.

Although Japan is fourth behind first-place USA for dog ownership (second, Brazil; third, China) with a little over 13 million dogs, they lavish affection on them to the sum of about 10 billion dollars a year. To the Japanese, their dog is a beloved family member, and owners of the spoiled canines buy them doggie clothes, take them for facials and massages, provide wheelchairs for senior pooches, and conduct elaborate funerals for them when they die.

According to a number of surveys, including the American Pet Products Association and the Humane Society of the United States, 39 million Americans own approximately 78.2 million dogs. Nearly 100 percent of the dog owners say that their pet provides them with companionship, love, company, and affection.

For 75 percent of dog owners, their dog is considered an integral part of their family, and they regard the pet as a child or a distinct family member.

Nearly 100 percent of dogs sleep inside their owners' dwelling. Sixty-five percent of dog owners allow their canine companion to sleep with them in their bed, duplicating the original nighttime sleeping arrangements when humans and dogs bunked down in caves. Of the remaining 35 percent of owners, nearly all have a special bed for their dog on the floor beside their own.

Nineteen percent of dog owners take the family dog with them on vacations or road trips.

A recent trend among dog lovers is the presentation of gifts to the pet on special occasions — or sometimes "just because." Surveys reveal that 88 percent of dog owners buy presents for their dog on birthdays, Christmas, Hanukkah, Easter, Halloween, and Valentine's Day. In addition to the presentation of gifts on those special days, 9 percent of dog owners invite other dog fanciers to attend parties "hosted" by their pets on their birthdays or on holidays.

One of the many reasons that we love dogs so much is that they make us feel good.

Dogs often make us laugh and help us to not take life too seriously — factors that definitely aid us in times of stress and tension.

The simple and natural act of petting your dog stimulates a soothing sensation of well-being. Dog owners have significantly reduced levels of risk factors for cardiovascular disease. Numerous international studies have found that dog owners have significantly lower levels of blood triglyceride, cholesterol, and systolic blood pressure.

A study at the School of Medicine at the State University of New York at Buffalo demonstrated that dogs can reduce stress in women even better than their best human friends could. While it is important to be able to turn to a good friend for comfort and advice, there are many special situations where women would rather turn to their dogs for nonjudgmental support.

Getting a dog can save your marriage, concluded a study at the University of Pennsylvania. Men and women struggling with a troubled marriage were less tense and angry when their dog was in the room. Studies at the University of Southern California School of Medicine agreed that having a dog can improve marriages, whether the couples were unhappy or very much in love. A dog is not critical or judgmental, so in its presence it is much easier for people to relax, to become more playful, to show affection — loving qualities that may then be transferred more readily to one's spouse.

Rebecca Johnson, a professor of nursing at the University of Missouri and director of the Research Center for Human-Animal Interaction, has conducted studies that indicate interactions with dogs produce multiple benefits, from lowered blood pressure to increased survival after heart attack.

Since the early 1990s, numerous documented cases of dogs being able to "sniff" out cancers in their owners in time for life-saving therapies have been established. Many medical researchers have documented dogs' ability to accurately predict oncoming epileptic seizures in their owners. Diabetic dog owners have also affirmed that their dogs can detect sharp falls in their blood sugar in sufficient time for them to ingest carbohydrates, thus preventing them from falling into hypoglycemic comas. Studies indicated that while none of the dogs displaying the ability to detect the approach of such seizures and comas had been trained to do so, experts theorize that dogs may be able to sense bioelectrical disturbances experienced by the human body.

According to Alan Beck, a veterinary professor with Purdue University's Center for the Human-Animal Bond, 40 percent of people who keep pictures of their spouse or children in their wallets also carry pictures of their pets with them. In today's society, Beck said, dogs and certain other pets are considered to be integral members of the American family.

In times past, owning a pet was considered a luxury that could be supported only by the more wealthy members of society. Farmers kept cats to keep their barns and storage sheds free of mice and were certain to have a dog to herd the cattle or to help protect the farm from nocturnal predators, but only the wealthy could afford to keep a dog solely as a companion. As the middle class in the United States grew, Beck said, more people had discretionary time and discretionary income. Pets became a part of the American home as full-fledged family members.

Stephen Zawistowski, science advisor to the American Society for the Prevention of Cruelty to Animals (ASPCA), noted that dog and pet ownership really began to soar after World War II as more people moved to the suburbs and had more room to keep dogs. As the U.S. population moved forward into the fifties and sixties, the picture of the typical household began to change. Motion pictures and television portrayed the American family as including a mom, dad, kids, and a dog and cat. Pets became an essential ingredient in the mix of the ideal American household.

In spite of pets having become beloved family members, the U.S. Humane Society, the Veterinarians Association, and the ASPCA have stated that as many as one dog is lost every five minutes. In 2011 an estimated 4 million dogs were lost or misplaced, and only 600,000 of that number were reclaimed at animal shelters. Those who have lost beloved dogs state that they found themselves in a boiling cauldron of painful emotions as the hours, days, and weeks passed without any signs of their dear friends.

Whether or not we have ever lost a dog, whenever we hear or read a dramatic and touching story about a dog finding its way home to a loving family across hundreds, even thousands, of miles, and sometimes after many years, even the most hard-nosed among us may mist up a bit.

And when a dog's love somehow enables it to work the miracle of locating its owner in faraway place, traversing areas where it has never been before, even the most skeptical and rational among us may be willing to concede that our canine companions may possess certain powers for which our present science simply has no explanation.

The authors of this book have each lost dogs, and we are sorry to report that in our personal stories, there were no happy endings. However, such losses, sad and tearful at the time, never prevented us from acquiring new canine friends who have enriched our lives and enabled us to feel closer to nature and to the Great Spirit who oversees all creatures.

All the stories in this book have happy endings. There may be some dangerous situations to be conquered, some great distances to be traversed, some frightening opponents to be thwarted, some impossible odds to overcome, some tears to be shed along the way, but we can sincerely promise that all of the lost dogs in this book do come home.

CHAPTER 1
DOGS THAT FOUND
THEIR WAY BACK HOME

"LASSIE COME HOME" STORIES

Many readers are familiar with the story of Lassie, the stalwart collie, who against seemingly impossible odds found her way back to her young owner. Based on a short story by Eric Knight published in *The Saturday Evening Post* in 1938, Lassie was more fully developed in Knight's novel *Lassie Come Home* in 1940. The storyline of the very successful 1943 motion picture *Lassie Come Home* tells of a Depression-era English family who is forced to sell their exceptionally beautiful female collie to a wealthy nobleman who lives hundreds of miles away on his estate in Scotland. Through a series of harrowing adventures, Lassie uses her instinct and courage and manages to return to the young boy she loves.

The film starred a teenage Roddy Mc-Dowall, an eleven-year-old Elizabeth Taylor, and a large male collie named Pal. Beginning with Pal I, the character of Lassie has always been portrayed by a male. (It was discovered early on in filming *Lassie Come Home* that female collies shed profusely when they are in heat.) Elizabeth Taylor got the part of Priscilla when Maria Flynn, the actress originally cast, could not conceal her fear of the big collie. Elizabeth had no problem working with Pal and did not find his size intimidating. Her father had given her a puppy when she was just a little girl, and she loved dogs — a love that continued throughout her life with spaniels, Pekingese, Maltese, Lhasa apsos, and collies. On her sixtieth birthday, Elizabeth was gifted with a collie that was a great-grandchild of Pal, her Lassie co-star.

In 1945, MGM capitalized on its canine bonanza with *Son of Lassie,* starring Peter Lawford and June Lockhart. The third movie in the series *Courage of Lassie,* in 1946, starred Tom Drake and Elizabeth Taylor, this time as Kathie Merrick. In this film, Lassie comes home battle-scarred after having served in the K-9 Corps in World War II.

In the *Lassie Radio Show* (1946–49) and in the long-running television series *Lassie* (1954–73), the collie didn't have to find her way home, but in each episode she faced a challenge on the farm that would stymie most adult humans. Tommy Rettig and June Lockhart are two actors most commonly associated with the series, which was later syndicated as *Jeff's Collie.*

Lassie had undeniably achieved popular culture immortality. In the 1980s and 1990s there were Lassie series produced by various production companies. In 1997 the Animal Planet network in the U.S. and Canada created a Lassie series that ran until 1999. In 2005 a United Kingdom production company did a remake of the original *Lassie Come Home,* starring Peter O'Toole and Samantha Morton. In that same year, *Variety* named Lassie one of the Top 100 Icons of All Time, thereby firmly establishing a "Lassie come home" story as a generic sobriquet for accounts of lost and found dogs.

BOBBIE, THE WONDER COLLIE OF OREGON, AND HIS THREE-THOUSAND-MILE TREK

In North America, perhaps the most famous of all the dogs who found their way back to the homes and hearts of their owners after conquering seemingly insurmountable distances and inhospitable environments is

Bobbie the collie, who made his way alone and on foot from Indiana back to his home in Oregon. With only his canine instincts to guide him, Bobbie managed to find his human family after walking three thousand miles through forests and farmlands, mountains and plains, scorching heat and freezing cold.

Bobbie's story is also fully documented. Although no one can fully know what trials and terrors the brave collie faced, endured, and conquered, when Colonel E. Hofer, president of the Oregon Humane Society, launched an investigation of Bobbie's fantastic journey, he received hundreds of letters from men and women who had assisted or befriended the dog on his amazing trek westward.

In their personal accounts, people remembered Bobbie because of his bobbed tail, the prominent scar over his right eye (where a horse had kicked him), his mismatched hips (after being struck by a tractor), and his three missing front teeth (torn out by their roots while he was digging for a ground squirrel). Some of these kind strangers had tended to Bobbie when he was starving, when he was freezing to death, when the pads of his toes were worn away so badly that the bone was exposed in some places.

It was from such reports that Charles D. Alexander, an author of short stories and novels for children, was able to document the story of the courageous dog in his book *Bobbie: A Great Collie of Oregon* (1926). The author of more than two hundred short stories and eleven books, mostly fiction, Alexander admitted that if he had not had access to such extensive documentation, the adventures of Bobbie would have seemed like the product of an unrestrained imagination.

The remarkable story of Bobbie's odyssey began in August 1923 when Mr. and Mrs. Frank Brazier, owners of a restaurant in Silverton, Oregon, began their long automotive journey to Indiana to visit relatives. Bobbie, their canine family member, rode on top of the luggage in the backseat of the open touring car.

Deciding to visit relatives in Wolcott, Indiana, before continuing a hundred miles farther east to Bluffton, their final goal, Frank drove the car with Bobbie in tow to a garage for a carburetor adjustment. As the big collie leaped from the backseat, he accidentally ran afoul of a formidable bull terrier.

Frank had no real concern for Bobbie as the collie and bull terrier stood sniffing and growling at each other. He couldn't imagine the two dogs actually getting into a fight, and if they did, he would soon break it up.

But what Frank didn't know was that the grumpy bull terrier had a whole pack of canine buddies who ganged up on Bobbie just as soon as they lured the collie out of sight of his watchful owner and the garage attendants. When Bobbie saw that the odds were seven or eight to one, he beat it out of town with the pack of growling, snapping dogs at his heels.

When the work on his automobile was completed, Frank drove up and down the town's streets and the nearby country roads, sounding the horn to summon Bobbie. The big dog would always come bounding for the backseat at the sound of the car horn. But not this time.

The next day, the Braziers placed an ad in the local paper, offering a reward for the return of their dog, and they delayed their drive to Bluffton to await what they prayed would be favorable results.

No response. No one seemed to have seen the big collie.

The Braziers knew that Bobbie would not run off. He was devoted to Frank. The

Braziers could only conclude that something terrible had happened to the collie while their automobile was undergoing minor repairs or that someone was keeping Bobbie against his will.

Bobbie had managed to escape pursuit from the inhospitable curs, but he was left confused, shaken, and frightened. He was in completely unfamiliar territory. He wanted only to return to his master — but where the heck was he?

The Braziers finally drove on to Bluffton, hoping that someone would soon spot Bobbie and bring him to their relatives in Wolcott. But when they returned there many days later, they were disheartened to learn that no one in that community had reported seeing a big collie anywhere in town or country.

They had no choice but to begin the long, sad drive back to Silverton, Oregon. It just wouldn't be the same without Bobbie in back, perched atop the luggage. And it wouldn't be at all the same without Bobbie in their lives, but it appeared that Bobbie was lost to them forever.

We can only imagine, from the collie's perspective, that he was at a loss to imagine why his master was nowhere in sight. Why hadn't he waited for him at the garage? He wasn't even able to pick up Frank's scent.

The problem was, the collie had become so disoriented that he headed in the opposite direction from Wolcott and was approaching garages that had never contained the scent of Frank Brazier or his automobile.

While Bobbie's sense of direction may have been temporarily skewered, his seemingly preternatural ability to detect dog lovers remained in excellent working order. Time and time again, as he was nearing starvation from walking in circles, Bobbie arrived at the home of kind people who took him in and nurtured him back to good traveling condition.

After more than a week of wandering, Bobbie appeared to have been given a renewed sense of direction and purpose. From what researchers could piece together, it was somewhere near Des Moines, Iowa, that Bobbie was done with walking in circles. He would keep to a westward course and never turn east again.

Traveling ever westward back home to Oregon, he swam rivers, survived blizzards, endured hunger and thirst, and climbed over mountains.

Nearly seven months later, a battered and worn Bobbie nudged past Mrs. Brazier and her daughter and dashed up the stairs to jump onto the bed where Frank lay sleeping after working the night shift at his restaurant. The startled man awakened to find his beloved collie licking his face and emitting howls of joy. Bobbie refused to leave his master's bedroom that day, even to accept food and water.

While not enough can be said about the collie's incredible endurance and survival, it is perhaps most astounding to learn that when the complete account had been pieced together and Bobbie's trail had been plotted on actual maps of the states that he had traversed, it was discovered that the dog had managed to pick a very reasonable route with very few detours. After the initial period of confusion and misdirection, it seemed as though Bobbie somehow had been given a precise mental "map" that would take him home.

What some dog owners also find remarkable is that even after surviving that three-thousand-mile trek through snow, freezing cold, and icy rivers, Bobbie enjoyed another three years with his beloved family in Silverton, Oregon.

Those years, however, were spent in quiet rest and relaxation. Bobbie had become a celebrated hero to the people of Oregon. He received medals and keys to cities at numerous local fairs and celebrations. He was the guest of honor at the Portland Home Show, where more than forty thousand people came to see him presented with his own dog-size cabin. On one occasion, Bobbie was awarded a jewel-studded harness and collar.

It was hardly surprising that Robert Ripley wrote about Bobbie in one of his famous "Believe It or Not!" columns, which was circulated throughout the United States and the world. The intrepid collie even played himself in a silent film entitled *The Call of the West,* a reel of which is preserved in the archives of the Oregon Historical Society Research Library.

When Bobbie passed away in 1927, he was buried with honors at the Oregon Humane Society. The mayor of Portland delivered the eulogy, and Rin Tin Tin, the wonder dog of Hollywood films, laid a wreath at his grave.

MIDGE FOUND HER WAY HOME AFTER BEING LEFT BEHIND ON A FAMILY OUTING

Dogs' legendary sense of smell and good memory may also have been the deciding factors in Midge being able to find her way back to her home forty miles away after being left behind on a family outing. David Van Slyke, a former high school physics teacher in Ohio, who ably serves as our webmaster, shared a cherished family story about a lost dog that found her way home. In Dave's own words:

The year is 1930. Herbert Hoover is president of the United States. My mother is eight years old and living in Wesleyville, Pennsylvania, with her parents, older brother, and Midge, a small mixed-breed dog. Several times a year, the family would drive their Model A Ford from Wesleyville to North Kingsville, Ohio, a distance of about forty miles, to visit Mom's grandmother at her farm in North Kingsville. The Model A had only one seat inside the car, plus a rumble seat in the back. That didn't matter to Midge because she preferred to ride outside, between the right front fender and the engine cowling. There was a flat space between the engine cowling and fender that was just right for a small dog. When the family would get ready to take the trip to Grandma's, my grandfather would call Midge and she would jump onto the front of the car and make herself comfortable in her special spot, facing forward so she could enjoy the view.

All these trips from Wesleyville to North Kingsville were uneventful, except one. On one of the visits, Midge missed her ride home. While the family visited inside Grandma's large farmhouse, Midge went off to romp in the woods. When it came time to leave, Midge was nowhere to be seen. The family went in different directions, calling for Midge. They looked for an hour or more and there was no sign of her. They wanted to get home by dark, and Grandma assured them that Midge would be fine and would come back to the house when she was ready. Grandma said she would call them as soon as Midge returned. The family reluctantly got in the Model A and went back to Wesleyville without Midge. As soon as they got home, they called Grandma. No sign of Midge.

They called twice a day for four days. Each time, Grandma told them sadly that there was no sign of Midge. Things weren't looking good. Then, on the fifth day, Midge showed up at our home in Wesleyville, barking at the side door, asking to come in. She was hungry and needed a bath, but was otherwise healthy.

Midge is the only one who knew the full story and she wasn't talking. She apparently had played in the woods a little too long and, upon returning to the house, noticed her ride, the Model A, was gone and took off for home on her own. We will never know whether she retraced the route she was so familiar with — through North Kingsville, east through Conneaut, Girard, Fairview, and Erie, and then south to Wesleyville — or took a more direct route. One thing we do know is that she must have used that internal GPS system so many animals, including dogs, seem to be equipped with.

Midge lived many years after her big adventure and took many more trips to Grandma's house on the front of the Model A.

STUBBY'S COURAGEOUS EIGHTEEN-MONTH, THOUSAND-MILE TREK TO RETURN TO DELIA

Stubby's eighteen-month, thousand-mile trek from the Indiana–Illinois border to his home in Colorado Springs, Colorado, was especially poignant because his thirteen-year-old mistress, Della Shaw, had been crippled and mute since birth. Stubby, Della's constant companion, had been the sunshine of her life until he vanished one terrible day in 1948.

Della and her grandmother, Mrs. Harry McKinzie, had been visiting relatives in Indianapolis on an extended four-month stay. Upon the completion of their visit, they had set out for home in a truck containing some furniture. Somewhere along the way, most likely between Indianapolis and Decatur, Illinois, Stubby had become separated from their vehicle.

The grief that a dog lover suffers when a cherished companion is lost may well be compounded in the heart of a handicapped child. Although Della was mute, her grandparents could feel so powerfully her silent sorrow over the loss of her devoted Stubby.

Harry McKinzie took out newspaper ads in cities along the route taken home by his wife and granddaughter. He contacted several friends to ask for their assistance in attempting to locate the missing dog.

Months passed without any results, and the McKinzies speculated that Stubby may have fallen from the truck and been killed. Della had slowly begun to adjust to life without Stubby. She was valiantly attempting to overcome the terrible loneliness that had been in her heart. The flurry of activities involved in moving to another house had also served as a distraction from awful thoughts of her Stubby being mangled on the highway.

In March of 1950, eighteen months after Stubby's disappearance on the ill-fated trip from Indianapolis, Harry McKinzie happened to walk by their old house. Incredibly, there was Stubby sitting on the sidewalk, staring vacantly into space, as if awaiting some command or signal.

The dog was dirty and dazed, his body bloated from hunger. His paws were swollen and bleeding, painful testament to some hard traveling on his long journey home.

Although Stubby seemed to scarcely recognize McKinzie, it was an entirely different story when he was brought to Della. The dog pushed himself free of McKinzie's grasp and excitedly began to lavish his mistress with soft whines and doggy kisses. Della wept with joy that some miracle had returned Stubby to her arms.

McKinzie told the International News Service on April 5, 1950, that Della was happy once again. "We can tell by the look on her face," he said. "And once Stubby gets all the food and sleep he needs, he'll be his old self again."

THE INCREDIBLE
HOMING INSTINCT IN DOGS

Dr. Nicholas Dodman theorized in his article "Homing Behavior in Dogs and Cats" that in their evolution with humans, the dog who could find his way home would be the dog most likely to survive and pass his genes on to his descendants. Like birds, the species most known for its ability to navigate vast distances, dogs may bring particular talents to bear on finding their way home, such as mental mapmaking; surveillance of the terrain; sense of smell; hearing (for example, recognizing the sound of a river); magnetic fields (dogs, like birds, may possess super-paramagnetic particles in their brains); and the position of the sun.

In *Psychology Today* (March 1, 2010), Lee Charles Kelly suggests that when a dog is lost and wants to find his way home, he does so not by remembering the route or by navigating by certain signposts or by thinking about finding his way home. To think about being lost and trying to remember where home is may be counterproductive. If a dog associates "home" with positive experiences such as comfort, food, love, and affection, the lost dog feels his way and goes by sensitivity to some natural kind of energy field — emotional, bioenergetic, cardiomagnetic, or morphogenetic — that allows him to plug into his internal GPS system.

"If home and family have any kind of emotional resonance for dogs — and I'm pretty sure they do — then it's *those* properties that displace the lost dog and pull him in one direction, not another," Kelly writes. "After all, there is a great deal of truth to the homily that 'home is where the heart is,' and of all God's creatures, dogs may be the ones with the most 'heart.' "

BEAR FINDS HIS WAY HOME AFTER SIX YEARS MISSING

Two days before Thanksgiving in 2003, Jeanie Flores of Wichita, Kansas, looked out the window of her home and felt a sudden rush of commingled joy and sadness. There, standing outside, was a dog that looked just like Bear, her dear brindle hound–Lab-chow mix, who had disappeared six years ago, just a few days before Thanksgiving in 1997.

The dog looked so much like Bear that she felt in her heart that the dog just had to be the pet that had vanished about a month after she and her husband, Frank, moved to a new neighborhood. But, she kept asking herself, how could it be? Where could Bear have been for six years? Why hadn't the brindle hound part of him with the ultra-powerful nose tracked them down before so much time had passed?

She had let him out of the house that night six years ago, and although she called and called his name, Bear did not come home.

She remembered how she sat up all night waiting for him, checking the door every few minutes to see if Bear was standing there on the steps, wanting to be let into the house.

But he never returned.

Frank and Jeanie were especially distressed because they had not yet updated Bear's ID tag with their new address. They'd gotten Bear in 1990 when he was just a puppy. They could not imagine his running away from them after being their pet for seven years.

In desperation, the Flores family followed the usual procedures for an all-out attempt to find a lost dog. Sherry Morse wrote in *Animal News* (December 13, 2003) that the Floreses put up signs and flyers, ran ads in the local newspaper, and from time to time they would drive around their old neighborhood.

But Bear had disappeared. He had disappeared until — dare she think it — today, almost six years to the day that he had vanished.

She stepped out of the house and called his name. Immediately, the dog responded with a whine. He was in pretty bad shape. His paws were torn and looked raw and bleeding in spots.

One of the Floreses' neighbors came out to watch the improbable family reunion. She told Jeanie that she had seen the big dog earlier in the day. It seemed as though he was carefully scrutinizing the houses before he finally approached the correct one.

Jeanie Flores was convinced that Bear had returned to them, and she called her husband at his place of work. As she was describing the dog standing outside their home, she began to cry, and Frank said that he would be home as soon as possible.

When Frank arrived home, he took one good look at the brindle hound–Lab-chow mix and agreed with his wife. Bear had come home for Thanksgiving.

As soon as an appointment could be made, Frank took Bear to a veterinarian to be examined. Frank explained that Bear had just come back home after a six-year absence and he wanted to be certain that their dear friend was well.

After the veterinarian had completed the examination, he assured Frank that Bear had not been mistreated or abused. He weighed only one pound less than when he had disappeared.

The only injuries Bear had sustained were those red and sore paws. It could only be theorized that the dog had been kept by someone for those six years until, one day, Bear decided that he wanted to go back home to the Floreses. Somehow, he must have broken out of the place where he was being held and pounded the pavement until his paws were raw, and until he located the Floreses' home in the new neighborhood.

Bear quickly readjusted to his family, who welcomed him back into the fold. The only dramatic adjustment to be made was for him to become acquainted with the Floreses' son, who had not yet been born when Bear disappeared.

ARE DOGS' MEMORIES OF THEIR HUMAN FAMILIES "STUCK IN TIME"?

Although the Floreses could recall to the day when their Bear vanished from their lives, could their errant dog do the same? Did Bear have any concept of how long he had been missing from the family who loved him so much?

Very little research has been done regarding a dog's concept of the passing of time. Many dogs appear to know when their owner usually comes home from work each day or when the kids come home from school. Dogs also seem to know when mealtimes should occur or when it is time for their daily walk, but there is no way of knowing if family dogs perceive time in the same way that their owners do — that is, being aware, for instance, that these events occur at four o'clock or six o'clock.

Although in many ways time is relative for us as humans, we all have the ability to remember events in the past and plan for events in the future. Time may be relative for us in some cases, such as Einstein's famous illustration that time spent with one's sweetheart and the same period of time spent in the dentist's chair are very different in perception, but, generally, we are mostly aware of the sequence of events that mark the passage of time.

Researcher William Roberts ("Are Animals Stuck in Time?" *Psychological Bulletin,* Vol. 128(3), May 2002) suggests that dogs may be "stuck in time" without the mental acuity it requires to form memories of the past or to project thoughts of the future.

Dogs, therefore, live only in the present and cannot mentally time travel backward and forward.

Dog owners may dispute this theory by reminding Roberts and other researchers of how well their dog is trained to perform certain tasks, actions learned in the past and remembered in the present. Researchers agreeing with Roberts counter this argument by stating their position that while a dog responds to commands, it does not have the specific memory of how that task was first learned. Researchers also point out that dogs do not appear to have the ability to plan for specific future events, but, again, seem to live in the present.

Perhaps when it comes to finding its way home, the dog may be far better off living in the present and relying upon its vast array of superior senses. It may be a uniquely human facet to have developed an understanding of time. However, it should be pointed out that no scientist would declare that he or she truly understands what the dimension of time really is.

British biologist Rupert Sheldrake's controversial *Dogs That Know When Their Owners Are Coming Home and Other Unexplained Powers of Animals* (1999) presents a database of sixty dogs that were taken to an unfamiliar location and then let loose to find their way back to their homes. The dogs were not given an opportunity to learn the smells or landmarks en route, and they typically followed a different route from the one over which they were transported. In addition to these remarkable "homing dogs," Sheldrake also discovered that not all dogs had the talent; some dogs headed in the wrong direction or sought forlorn refuge on the doorstep of the nearest home.

THE NOSE KNOWS — SOMETIMES

Some scientists and dog experts have suggested that in many cases of lost dogs that found their way home, the dogs may have been directed by their strong sense of smell. Smell is the dog's dominant sense, estimated to be 100,000 times better than a human's. The dog's wet snout acts like a sponge, catching even the most minute molecules of smells, and then dissolves them so the dog's internal smell receptor cells may analyze them correctly. To keep his nose sufficiently wet to perform this seemingly preternatural ability, a dog must produce a pint of mucus daily.

Dogs are particularly sensitive to the smell of fear, an alarm pheromone produced in the anal glands of frightened dogs. To a dog's powerful sense of smell, all humans have an individual, unique odor. According to scientists who conducted experiments with dogs' sense of smell, the only possible way that a dog wouldn't be able to tell two people apart would be if they were identical twins on an identical diet.

Dogs can track human smells over long distances and can pick up the differences in odors from different footprints. Incredibly, dogs can even smell human fingerprints left on objects up to a week later. As impossible as it may seem, a dog's nose is so sensitive that they can smell electricity by detecting tiny amounts of ozone.

The aroma of lavender and chamomile tends to make dogs calm, while rosemary and peppermint make them energized.

Under test conditions, dogs can detect cancer in humans with an accuracy rate of between 88 and 97 percent simply by sniffing samples of a subject's breath. The accuracy of a multimillion-dollar hospital scanner is between 85 and 90 percent.

A strong sense of smell may be what enabled Laser, a three-year-old beagle, to find his way home to the LePage family, who had adopted him only a month before he slipped his leash and ran away during a fireworks display at Lake Winnipeg on May

22, 2010. Parry LePage, who lives in Transcona, a suburb of Winnipeg, remarked that the family had really bonded with Laser in the four weeks that he had lived with them, which may certainly have been an important factor in Laser's being able to travel the fifty miles to find his way home from Winnipeg Beach to Transcona on July 5.

MIRACLE MAX MAY HAVE USED HIS MEMORY AND HIS NOSE TO GUIDE HIM HOME

Bill Clark of Coventry, Rhode Island, was driving in his convertible in Sterling, Connecticut, in September 2008 when he was struck by another car. The drivers were uninjured, and so apparently was Max, Clark's two-year-old Airedale terrier. Max must have been frightened and disoriented, for when he escaped the convertible through its trunk, he ran into the nearby woods.

Clark called for Max and looked in the immediate area, hoping to find the terrier crouching somewhere waiting for his human to find him and bring him home. For over three weeks, Max was nowhere to be found.

Some people claimed to have seen such a dog on the loose, but none of the leads proved to be fruitful. There were forty-five miles between Sterling and Coventry, and Bill Clark was beginning to fear that Max had set out to find his way home and had only become more and more disoriented and lost. Not knowing if it would help or not, Clark placed some of his clothing and some of Max's favorite food at various locations along the highway to help Max pick up the scent.

But Max proved to be a very resourceful terrier. Three weeks and three days after Max had gone missing, Clark returned home to find him sitting in the backyard. When their veterinarian examined Max, he said that he had lost eleven pounds. Bill Clark told WJAR (on October 2, 2008) that worrying over his beloved terrier had caused him to lose seven.

IT TOOK SEVEN MONTHS AND 550 MILES FOR BOSCO TO COME HOME*

Brian "Bud" Bitker got Bosco, a beagle pup, in the summer of 1996, between his sophomore and junior year in high school. Bud and Bosco had plenty of afternoons to bond

* At the request of the individuals involved in this story, names and places have been changed to protect their anonymity.

after Bud had finished helping his mother in the restaurant that she ran in the small Ohio town where they lived.

They had been a farm family until Bud's father passed away in 1995. Ellen Bitker, known throughout the county as a fantastic cook, bought the small restaurant in town in order to support herself and her son. The Bitkers had only been renting the farm, so after her husband, Lawrence, passed, Ellen and Bud got a house in town, and the landowner leased the place to another farmer.

The restaurant, Ellen's Kitchen, served breakfast and lunch Monday through Saturday, and dinner on Tuesday and Thursday nights. Such a schedule gave Bud plenty of opportunities to bring Bosco along to the swimming hole in warm weather and also allowed Bud the time to participate in high school sports. On Tuesday nights during the athletic season when Bud had a game, Ralphene and Gary Stokes, their former neighbors, would come in from their farm to fill in.

In 2000, Bud graduated from high school and made plans to attend Ohio State University Agricultural Technical Institute at Wooster. It had been Lawrence Bitker's dream that Bud would one day attend college and be a Buckeye, and he had established a savings account soon after his son's birth so that goal could be accomplished.

Bud told his mother that he planned to take Bosco with him to college, but when the day came in September for Bud to leave, reality set in and he had to concede what his mother and his friends had argued all along: Dogs wouldn't be welcome in dormitory rooms.

In spite of being "all grown up," Bud admitted that he had tears in his eyes when he drove away from the well-wishers who had come to see him off from Ellen's Kitchen. In the rearview mirror, he could clearly see a very sad and confused Bosco being held back by Ralphene Stokes.

Bud soon found himself and his thoughts completely occupied with his classes and the adjustment often experienced by students who come from small towns and small high schools to enter much larger establishments of higher education. And after a few bone-rattling series of impacts on the football field, he quickly discovered that he would not achieve the status of Friday Night Hero that he had enjoyed back home.

Since he did not make the cutoff and so did not make the football team, Bud did find time to drive home on an occasional weekend, and he was able to maintain quality time with Bosco during vacation periods. And there were the wonderful summers, working at the restaurant, spending time with Bosco, and even managing to work in steady dating with a girl who was attending a nearby community college.

In January 2002, during his sophomore year, shortly after he had been home for the Christmas holiday, his mother wrote Bud to let him know that she was going to visit his aunt Helen, her twin sister, in Tennessee for a few weeks. He was not to worry about Bosco. She would take him along. Ralphene and Gary Stokes would be running the restaurant while she was away.

The few weeks tragically grew to several months. Shortly after she had arrived at Aunt Helen's, Ellen was involved in a near-fatal accident. She was hospitalized for three weeks, and she would have to recuperate at her sister and brother-in-law's home for an undetermined length of time.

Bud flew down to see his mother while she was in the hospital, and he was saddened to see her all bound up in traction and in obvious pain and discomfort.

His aunt told him that he might as well face reality — it could be months before his mother could travel back to Ohio. He shouldn't worry about her. They had plenty of room in their home for her to recuperate.

When Bud asked about Bosco, his uncle Carleton told him that he and Bosco got along just fine. Carleton had always kept hounds until just the past few years. He would take really good care of Bosco.

Bud returned to college, trying to focus on his studies and desperately attempting not to worry about his mother and Bosco.

Things seemed to be progressing as well as could be hoped.

And then he received that terrible telephone call from his uncle.

Carleton had decided to take Bosco with him to go out hunting rabbits. As soon as he let Bosco off his leash to chase some rabbits, the beagle vanished. That was the last he saw of Bosco. And that was a week ago.

His uncle's words became awkward and apologetic as Bud heard how Carleton had put up signs and posters, placed ads in newspapers, called area veterinarians, and was doing all that he could.

Bud doesn't recall what he said before he hung up the telephone. He only remembers being struck with pangs of guilt and sorrow. His beloved Bosco, feeling rejected and confused, had run off into the woods of Tennessee, probably never to be seen again. It was many days before Bud could even begin to focus on his class work.

About a week later, Bud learned even worse news. Because it had seemed as though Bosco would be staying in Tennessee for quite some time and Carleton wanted to take him hunting, he had removed Bosco's Ohio dog tags. Carleton had responsibly acquired Tennessee tags, but he had forgotten to place them on Bosco before they went hunting. Without tags, Bosco would appear to be a stray dog on the loose. With this added depressing confession from Uncle Carleton, Bud somberly resigned himself to the grim reality that he would never see his beloved Bosco again.

In late August, Bud was flipping hamburgers in Ellen's Kitchen when he heard Ralphene calling his name. "Merciful heavens!" she was now shouting. "Bud, come look out the front door!"

There, leaning against the bench they kept alongside the entrance, was Bosco. He was painfully thin. His paws were worn and bleeding, but he was home.

Ralphene joined Bud in hugging and petting his beloved beagle. Bosco had become homesick and had set out on a 550-mile trek just as soon as he was able to get free of his leash. It had taken him seven months, but he had made it.

He was covered with ticks — and Bud saw that he was missing a chunk out of his left ear — but Bosco had come home.

A small crowd gathered around them, and Bud heard people expressing their awe and amazement that the tough little beagle had been able to survive and to conquer thunderstorms, heat, freezing cold, rivers, and mountains to walk the route from Tennessee to Ohio.

A visit to the local veterinarian confirmed that Bosco needed some tender loving care and some good grub, but he was in relatively good condition. The strange row of scars on his back caused the vet to theorize that Bosco had been raked by some large bird of prey, such as a hawk or a large owl.

Bud called his mother and told her the good news. After her squeals of joy had subsided, Bud had another announcement to make. It was nearly time for him to head back to Ohio State in Wooster, but he had decided to transfer to the local community college since they had recently added a four-year program in business. He had two good reasons to do so. He missed Bosco, who would now need his attention and care, and he also missed a certain young lady who attended the local community college.

SCOOBY RETURNED HOME
AFTER TWO MONTHS MISSING

On April 27, 2006, John Haga delivered his daughters, Isabelle and Olivia, to their grandparents in Grand Junction, Colorado. On his way back to Olathe, he decided to stop in the Escalante Canyon area, about sixteen miles from home, and go for a hike with the family's bloodhound, Scooby.

The Haga family had obtained Scooby from the local animal shelter, and the hound had quickly adapted to their home environment. Every member of the family loved Scooby, and he lavished his doggy affection on every one of them, so John had absolutely no reason to believe that once he released Scooby from the vehicle, the hound would take off like his tail was on fire. Before John had an opportunity to put a leash on Scooby's collar, the big dog was off and running.

There was no way that he could outrun the bloodhound, so John stood helplessly beside his motor vehicle and watched Scooby disappear into the wilderness of Escalante Canyon.

For a while, John thought that since they had been driving for quite some time, Scooby just wanted to stretch his legs, obey a call of nature, and would then come running back to the car to go for a hike with his owner.

No such luck.

After waiting a considerable period of time for this hopeful scenario to unfold, John Haga got back into his car and drove up and down the dirt road, looking for some sign of Scooby.

Several futile hours passed, and John decided that he had to return to Olathe with the sad news that Scooby had disappeared.

The family was devastated by the news that their beloved hound had run off and vanished into Escalante Canyon. They spent the next three days driving the dirt roads and walking the trails of the canyon, calling and searching for their dog.

The Haga family followed the standard prescribed procedure for finding a lost dog: They put up posters, notified animal shelters and veterinarians, and placed ads in newspapers.

Finally, they gave up all hope of ever seeing their Scooby again.

Then, after two months, Scooby came walking back into the yard of the Haga home in Olathe. His life as Lord of Escalante Canyon or as King of the Road had finally soured, and he was happy to return to the Haga hearth.

The Haga family welcomed their wandering hound back home. Scooby was considerably thinner, and he bore a bit of porcupine quill in his eye that would need surgery, but he was the same old bloodhound that they all loved.

MOON GOT SKUNKED BEFORE SHE FOUND HER WAY HOME

Doug Dashiell didn't mind that Moon, his beloved Siberian husky, smelled so bad that he could hardly get near her — he was just happy to see her again after she'd been missing for seven days. The pungent stench of skunk was overwhelming, but would wash out eventually with a few baths — well, maybe *quite* a few.

On April 6, 2008, during the return portion of a weekend trip to Tonopah, Nevada, Doug and his three dogs stopped at a rest stop on their way home to Ely, Nevada. Moon, a purebred Siberian husky, somehow broke loose when a link on her chain gave out. Not looking back for even a moment, she bolted into the sagebrush and took off, heading northwest in the direction of the Duckwater Shoshone Reservation.

Doug spent over two hours searching for Moon before giving up the search. He called the tribal police at the reservation, hoping to locate her there, only to be told there was no trace of her . . . yet.

Puzzling over why such a dear pet that he had cherished for one year and nine months would have taken off like that, Doug made the rest of the trek home, being extra attentive the entire way . . . just in case he might see Moon appear magically by the side of the road.

Upon arriving home, Doug comforted himself with the memories of when Moon had run away from home before, but always managed to return home within hours or a day or two at the most. Doug continued to make phone calls, inquiring throughout the entire area, and doing whatever else he thought might alert others to a missing dog.

As the days began to pass with no Moon in sight, trepidation soon sank in as Dashiell recognized this wasn't like those few other times Moon had run away from familiar territory; this was far different. Not only was the area in which she disappeared completely foreign to the frisky husky, it was exceedingly *rugged* terrain, over two mountain ranges, a river, and high desert — seventy-seven miles of it! Doug feared he would never see his beloved Moon dog again. By now, one week had passed. There had not been a single phone call or report of a sighting of her and certainly no message that she had been found.

According to John Plestina of the *Ely Times Reporter* (June 17, 2008), after she'd been missing for seven days, Dashiell suspected that Moon was either dead, had turned wild, or that someone might have found and kept her. Any hope he might have held on to had dwindled to zero.

Then, on the following Monday morning, there came a call from the White Pine Veterinary Clinic with information about a dog that had been spotted. On Sunday night, Alvin Molea found a beautiful albeit smelly dog . . . outside of R Place grocery store in Ely. A benevolent dog lover, he took her home and gave her a warm place to sleep. Then on Monday morning when Molea went to check on the dog, he noticed a dog tag around her neck that was from the White Pine Veterinary Clinic . . . so he called the number, describing the dog he'd picked up.

It had taken Moon one week to walk from the rest stop near Tonopah to Ely, a distance of nearly eighty miles, but she'd made it! Tom Sanders from the White Pine Veterinary Clinic was happy to tell Doug that Moon was back in town — a bit worse for wear, but in one piece and very, very stinky!

Apparently a skunk had let loose its signature scent, bathing Moon in its wretched, unmistakable trademark aroma. Perhaps Moon had even chased after it or its family and had it coming, from the skunk's perspective. No matter, Dashiell was ecstatic to be reunited with his Moon and figured she must have survived on wild rabbits during the time she was missing. She was slimmer, but not frail, and seemed in good physical shape. *How* she survived or made it home wasn't important. All that mattered was that she was safely home. Damage control could de-skunk Moon with as many baths as it would take to make her shine and smell "pretty" again.

CHAPTER 2
DOGS THAT WERE FREAKED BY THEIR NEW SURROUNDINGS

CHANGES ARE HARD ON DOGS, TOO

It is not uncommon for dogs to become disoriented after a move from a familiar residence to a new one — especially if that move takes them across the country. There are new surroundings, new smells, new sounds, and new neighbors, all of which may tax a sensitive dog's nervous system. A dramatic move can prove unsettling both to children and adults, who benefit from knowing the reason for a move and quite likely have participated in numerous discussions of why the move was necessary. In many cases, the family is so concerned with the adjustment of the human members to a new scene and circumstances that they may not give much thought or consideration to the idea that their canine companion may be terribly confused by the change of environment that must be accepted as a part of their strange new reality.

BUCA, THE MYSTERY DOG OF I-15

For two months in 2003, motorists driving I-15 near Orem, Utah, had their attention to the highway diverted by the sight of a mysterious black dog that sat atop a hill. From time to time, a concerned animal lover would alert the Orem Animal Control Shelter and report the lost dog perched on a knoll near the 800 North off-ramp.

More than a dozen motorists reported the dog, making such statements as "He seems to be watching for someone" or "It's as if he's looking for one particular car to drive by." After animal-control officers made a number of efforts to capture the large black dog, news items began to surface about the mystery dog of I-15.

When Debra Benson saw one of the media reports, she had an inner conviction that she knew the identity of the mystery dog — it was their Buca, missing for over two months.

Benson had brought Buca with her family when they moved from Tennessee to Orem, Utah, in December 2002. She had purchased the dog from a NASA rocket scientist over five years before. Buca was a member of a rare breed called Yodapei, and the Benson family thought that he looked just like a bear cub — hence his name,

Buca, "a cub" spelled backward. In spite of his size and his bold name, Buca was very shy and was strictly a one-owner family dog.

Shortly after Benson and her three children, ages eighteen, thirteen, and twelve, arrived in Orem, Buca suddenly ran out of the open door of her brother's garage. They all chased after him, calling his name and begging him to come back. Debra's brother continued to chase Buca deeper and deeper into the neighborhood until the dog seemed to disappear.

They had arrived just a few days before Christmas, and everyone expressed their terrible depression and how bad they would feel if Buca were not with them during the holiday. They spent three or four days searching for the dog and distributed more than a hundred "lost dog" flyers throughout the city. In addition, Debra visited every dog pound in town every day for a month.

This was so unlike Buca. The family commiserated and wondered why their precious pet would run away from them.

They recalled how quietly he had sat during the four-day drive from Tennessee. Buca had sat watching the cars zip by them, studying the highway intently, as if he might have to take over the wheel.

It was a very sad Christmas for the Benson family. Buca had become such an important and integral member of their family circle that the children could not bear to think of life without him. Kisses, their white West Highland terrier, so grieved for Buca that she refused to eat after Buca disappeared.

At the same time that Debra had such a firm feeling that the dog was their Buca, she was struck with the remarkable irony that she had driven by that very spot about fifteen times since Buca had disappeared. How bizarre that so many people had seen the dog except the one person who was looking for him.

There on the hill there was a flattened patch of grass where Buca sat and watched the cars, waiting for the Bensons to drive by so that he might rejoin them. Because he was so shy, Buca would run into a nearby orchard and evade pursuit whenever strangers or volunteers from the animal shelter had tried to catch him.

Debra Benson felt that because Buca had studied the highway so carefully, he knew that his family would come by eventually, and then he would emerge and they would all be happy once again. It is remarkable to consider that Buca was so loyal to the Bensons that he camped out on the hillside, faithfully awaiting someone from his family to find him, week after week resisting the calls and entreaties of strangers who sought to give him food and shelter.

After two months encamped on the hill, Jesse Hyde of the *Deseret News* (February 13, 2003) reported, the mystery dog of I-15 was at last reunited with the Bensons — and with his companion, Kisses the terrier.

BAILEY FOUND HIS WAY HOME AS FAST AS HIS LITTLE LEGS WOULD ALLOW

In our opinion, courage and endurance must always be considered a matter of perspective. For example, it may not be a very big deal for a healthy, two-year-old German shepherd to run or to trot seven miles to his owner's home, but place that same challenge before a ten-year-old bichon frisé no larger than a sofa throw pillow and the stakes become considerably higher.

In September 2007, Lou Staigvil, who lives in a suburb of Pittsburgh, decided to take Bailey, his bichon frisé, along on a firewood-splitting expedition at his sister's place about seven miles away in the country. Lou's sister had a gentle golden retriever that always played well with the older, smaller, fifteen-pound dog, and Bailey also loved to romp with the animal.

When the firewood-splitting chores were completed, however, it appeared that while the two dogs were playing, Bailey had wandered away and become lost. If only the golden retriever could speak and tell them what had lured Bailey away from the area in which they were supposed to stay — and in which direction he had headed.

Immediately a search party was organized. Surely, old Bailey could not have run away very far on those little old legs of his. He had to be somewhere near, perhaps chewing on an old bone that he had appropriated from the retriever.

After searching the area for hours, Lou Staigvil was faced with the unpleasant task of returning home without Bailey and attempting to explain to his wife, Janet, what he himself did not know: How could Bailey have gotten lost while they were splitting firewood? How could Bailey have disappeared when he was scarcely out of their sight for more than a few minutes?

The Staigvils ran off flyers and posted them in the area. They spent hours searching every neighborhood for miles around for any sign of their Bailey. The bichon frisé meant so much to them. After ten years of enjoying his peculiarities, quirks, and lovable traits, they were distraught at his loss.

After three days devoted almost entirely to searching for Bailey, they returned home to find the greatest gift for which they could ever wish waiting for them. Their ten-year-old companion was sitting on their front steps. He had walked the seven miles from Lou's sister's place to the Staigvil residence and found his own way home.

Lou's sister was relieved to learn that Bailey was home where he belonged, but she remarked to Paul Peirce of the *Tribune-Review* (September 26, 2007) that that was a lot of walking for something with such tiny legs.

Janet Staigvil said that those little feet of Bailey's were pretty sore, but he seemed too happy to be home to complain.

Friends observed that a doggy angel must have kept watch over Bailey. The bichon frisé was not really streetwise, and he would have had to have walked on or near some very busy highways, country roads, and some big-city streets to have found his way safely home.

A CANINE COLLISION AT A DOG SHOW SPOOKED HONOR

Canine collisions are certainly not unheard of at dog shows. When many dogs and their handlers are running around the judging circle or being led to the grooming stalls, accidents can and do happen — and no one makes a big fuss about them. It is just a small aspect of what can go wrong at any event, regardless of how well it may be planned.

But on May 12, 2007, at the Georgia National fairgrounds in Perry, Honor, a Portuguese water dog, got so spooked when another dog fell on her that she took off running toward the woods. Rindi Gaudet, Honor's handler, ran after her, thinking that she would easily catch the dog after it had calmed down, but she soon discovered that Honor was nowhere to be seen.

Perhaps because Honor was still basically a pup at eleven months old, she may have believed that the other dog was attacking her. Regardless of the pup's rationale for fleeing the judging area, she had disappeared.

After waiting for several hours after the judging was completed and still no Honor, Rindi Gaudet and Corey Krickeberg, Honor's other handler, decided that they would drive back to Fayetteville, South Carolina, that evening and return the next day to search the area for the dog. They agreed that they would search for Honor all week if that was what it would take.

Incredibly, the search became eight days of exhaustive walking through woods and urban neighborhoods. No one would guess that the well-trained pup could have been so frightened that she would head for the woods and hide out for such a long period of time. Gaudet, Krickeberg, other dog handlers, and members of the community spent a solid week hunting for the lost Portuguese water dog. Rindi Gaudet and Honor's owners were becoming so concerned that they discussed issuing a thousand-dollar reward for information leading to the dog's return.

Finally, on Sunday, May 20, eight days after Honor disappeared, Rindi Gaudet received a telephone call from two mechanics in Perry who had spotted the dog on Marketplace Road. They managed to lure her into a gated area from which she could not run away, and they said that they would watch her until someone could come and get her.

Because Rindi was the closest of Honor's handlers, she immediately left Fayetteville to drive to Perry to make a positive identification.

It was Honor, and she seemed happy to be back in Rindi Gaudet's care.

Realizing that Honor had probably had no food and little water for many days, Rindi drove the pup directly to their local veterinarian in Fayetteville. Incredibly, after eight days without food, water, or shelter, Honor was found to be in good condition, and the vet gave her a clean bill of health.

Afterward, speaking on behalf of Honor's owners and the other handlers, Rindi thanked all those who had helped return her to their care. As noted in *Dogster Lifestyle* (May 30, 2007), they could not have found their precious Honor without the help of many unselfish individuals.

KOKOMO SURVIVED TWENTY-FOUR DAYS IN SUBZERO TEMPERATURES

The winter months of 1994 will be remembered as particularly brutal in the New England and Eastern Seaboard states. Night after night, the temperatures dipped into the bone-chilling subzero range. Those were not fit nights out for man nor beast, but those were the frigid days and nights when Kokomo, a twelve-year-old shepherd mix, chose to undergo her twenty-four-day ordeal.

The strange saga began on a night in early January when Carolyn and Terry Powers asked Terry's parents in East Meadow, Long

Island, to "dogsit." When they returned to reclaim their faithful old shepherd, it became chillingly apparent that Kokomo had not really understood the plan of being with dogsitters. Sometime while the Powerses were enjoying an evening out, the dog had jumped a three-foot chain-link fence and run away.

The Powers family conducted an extensive two-week search for Kokomo. They put up posters, placed notices in local newspapers, and contacted humane and animal care agencies in the area — all to no avail. They were all brokenhearted over the loss of their dog, especially the kids, Sean and Kelly.

But then, at 3:30 A.M., twenty-four days after she had disappeared, a very bedraggled and nearly frozen Kokomo appeared at the Powerses' home in West Islip, New York, weakly barking at their door, asking to be let in to love and warmth.

The Powers family will never know why Kokomo ran away from Terry's parents to undergo a freezing hell on the run for more than three weeks. She returned to them as a shivering skeleton that had lost at least fifteen of her forty-five pounds.

Carolyn Powers recalled that as soon as they opened the front door to the half-frozen Kokomo, she crawled straight under the bed.

BOSCOE DISAPPEARED
FOR FIFTEEN DAYS

The first time that Kelly Sugarman saw the picture of a shar-pei named Boscoe on the Web site of the Worcester Animal Rescue, she fell in love with him.

Many dog lovers will tell you that shar-peis are kind of an acquired taste. The very name means "sandy coat," and the dog's hair feels like sandpaper when you try to pet it. Of course, the first thing you notice about a shar-pei is that it looks like it is wearing a coat four times too large for it. The dog was bred in China to fight and to guard, so having a hide so full of wrinkles around its head, neck, and shoulders allows it to more easily twist away from the teeth of an attacker. Some say the shar-pei existed as early as 200 BCE, and most authorities recognize the "wrinkled" dog's existence beginning in the thirteenth century — though no one claims to know its exact origins. The breed did not arrive in the United States until the late 1960s, and experts warned that the breed tottered closely upon the brink of extinction.

All that being noted, Kelly Sugarman loved shar-peis, and as she looked at

Boscoe's picture on the Wrinkled Rescue of Ohio (WRO) Web site, she was reminded of the dear shar-pei she had lost to cancer. A representative of the WRO told Kelly that Boscoe had been abused and that he didn't like men. In addition, he would also require eye and mouth surgery.

Kelly took that slightly negative information in stride. She had always loved shar-peis. In fact, at the time that she was making arrangements to acquire Boscoe, she already had three shar-peis living comfortably in the Sugarman home.

In May 2007, David and Kelly Sugarman adopted Boscoe and set about making his life a great deal better than it had ever been. The Sugarmans reside in Princeton, Massachusetts, but Kelly spent the summer on Cape Cod with Boscoe and the other three shar-peis.

Kelly returned to Princeton after Labor Day with her four shar-peis, her faithful traveling companions. On the evening of September 9, Kelly told writer Phyllis Booth (*Dogomaniak,* March 2008), Boscoe had been walking behind her, following her to her car, when something in the woods startled him, and he left her side to pursue whatever he had sensed in the darkness. Boscoe was not yet familiar with the residence and the surrounding area in Princeton; regardless, Kelly was not troubled by the strange noise, but she became truly concerned for him when she realized that, since Boscoe's coat was black, she couldn't see in which direction he went after he entered the wooded area. Doubling the problem was the number of cars speeding by that would be unable to see a black dog suddenly jumping out of the trees onto the highway.

She called his name again and again, hoping to see him come lumbering out of the woods, but she got no response.

On the one hand, she was not particularly frightened for Boscoe physically. He could probably take good care of himself against a coyote or another dog. He weighed about fifty pounds, and by his very breeding he was a fighting dog, capable of being aggressive and protecting himself.

On the other hand, she worried that a pack of coyotes or wild dogs might gang up on her poor Boscoe, who was still really not completely up to peak form after his eye and mouth surgery. Poor Boscoe. They had adopted him to make his life better, not to make it worse.

But now he had suddenly disappeared in the darkness.

In the next few days, Kelly ran off hundreds of "lost dog" posters. In addition, she called local and state police departments, dog pounds, veterinarians, even middle schools and high schools to let them know that a shar-pei named Boscoe was lost somewhere in the heavily wooded area between Route 62 in Princeton and Route 31 in Holden.

The Craft Center in Worcester, where Kelly worked, gave her time off to search for Boscoe, and one day her boss even took off work to help Kelly and David comb the woods near their home.

Kelly spent many hours searching the area herself. She was aware that there were a number of good people out in the woods looking for Boscoe, but she also knew that because of his former abuse and his fear of men, he was likely to run away from the searchers rather than toward them.

Three days after Boscoe went missing, Kelly received a telephone call from a man who was certain that he had seen the shar-pei about a mile into the woods.

Kelly left immediately, spent more than three hours searching in the area that the caller had described, and ended up nearly getting lost herself. How ironic to become lost while searching for a missing dog.

A few days later, on the advice of a dog trainer, Kelly set up a tent in the woods and stayed there for hours, hoping that Boscoe would catch her scent and approach her. Finally admitting failure at another method of summoning her dog, Kelly folded up her tent and returned home.

The Sugarmans continued to receive telephone calls from individuals who claimed to have seen Boscoe in various places between Princeton and Holden.

One kind woman even spent the morning walking with Kelly in the rain on a section of Wood Road, pointing out the places where she was certain that she had sighted Boscoe.

It seemed as though the long search may at last have ended when the Sugarmans got a call from a motorcyclist who had seen Boscoe sitting in the middle of the road. The man was certain that it was Boscoe because he had seen his picture on so many flyers posted around the area.

When they arrived at the place the motor-cyclist described, Kelly felt her heart beat faster. There was her dear Boscoe, sitting beneath a streetlight. Following all the advice that she had received from dog train-ers and animal rescue personnel, Kelly ap-proached the shar-pei very slowly, calling his name in a soft and gentle voice.

She was crushed and despondent when Boscoe turned and ran back into the woods.

The days and nights were passing. It had been nearly two weeks since the startled Boscoe had run off into the darkness of the woods off Coal Klin Road and disappeared.

Kelly refused to consign her dog to the slow death of starvation or the cruel death of wild animal attack. She renewed her efforts to find Boscoe by distributing more posters and flyers. She even baited one of her lookout posts with a freshly cooked chicken in an attempt to lure him to her.

On the fifteenth day Boscoe was missing, Kelly received a call from Animal Companion Retrievable Company with good news, tinged with bad. Boscoe had been found by a couple in the woods near their Holden home. He had been identified by the microchip under his skin. The bad news was that Boscoe had been struck by a car, which was the reason why he had not been able to run away when approached by the couple.

Kelly drove immediately to the home where Boscoe lay injured. She was unable to hold back the tears when she saw how thin the shar-pei had become. Boscoe's muzzle spouted porcupine quills, silent testimony of an encounter with a prickly denizen of the woods, and it was obvious that he had sustained serious injuries to his legs from being struck by the automobile.

After thanking the couple for finding her precious Boscoe, Kelly loaded him into her car and took him to a veterinary hospital, where a surgeon found three breaks in his left leg and a dislocated right hip. Boscoe would receive surgery and spend the next few days on IV fluids in the animal hospital.

Back home with the Sugarmans, Boscoe was placed on pain medication and antibiotics. Although perhaps it had not been specifically prescribed, they decided that Boscoe should have an extra meal a day to bring his emaciated body back up to a healthier weight. The veterinarians also applied a sling under his legs that he would have to wear for the next few weeks.

Kelly Sugarman told writer Phyllis Booth that they were so grateful to the many good people of the area who helped them recover their very special Boscoe.

RAYMOND LEARNED A VALUABLE LESSON: BE CAREFUL WHO YOU ASK TO WATCH YOUR DOG

Raymond (not his real name) wrote to tell us of his experience with his lost cocker spaniel, Buster, that occurred while he was a student living in Costa Mesa, California. Moved by his story, we asked him to write to us again, providing us with more details.

After graduating from high school in 1997, Raymond could not afford to attend college. His father had passed away when Raymond was in junior high, and his mother, who had supported the family by working as a secretarial temp, had grown quite ill during his senior year. Raymond's older sister was working her own way through college and could not spare a dime to help him with tuition. Assuming personal responsibility, Raymond entered the workforce as a timberman with a logging company in Oregon and saved his money so that he could afford to go to college full-time in 2001, to study business administration.

After a few years, he was able to move into an apartment in town, and he got Buster, a cocker spaniel puppy, to keep him company. Raymond said that it was amazing how much the dog came to mean to him. When he was a kid, his family could never afford a dog. "We could barely feed ourselves, and I can't think of too many meals where there would have been any scraps to nourish a dog," Raymond said. "Even the barest scraps left by any meal were called 'leftovers,' and used by Mom in some casserole or stew for the next dinnertime."

Raymond found a very nice apartment complex that allowed pets, and he and Buster moved into an attractive first-floor apartment just in time for Raymond to enroll in one of the local colleges. Buster was used to waiting for Raymond to return home after late hours working in the forests of Oregon, so the cocker spaniel was thrilled by his owner's new schedule that allowed him to come home sometimes in the early afternoon. Tuesdays and Thursdays meant time to drive out to the countryside and really get to run. Mondays, Wednesdays, and Fridays were times to romp around the neighborhood and learn about traffic and automobiles.

Raymond couldn't help noticing an attractive brunette who enjoyed soaking up as much sunshine around the complex's swimming pool as her class schedule would allow. Early, tentative conversations had provided him with the information that Carol was taking a light class load because she, too, had to work her way through college. She worked nights as a waitress and was majoring in art.

Although Raymond would occasionally swim laps at the pool, he had had enough of the sun and outdoor living those years in the Oregon forests, so sunbathing held no attraction for him. However, he wouldn't deny that *Carol* held some attraction for him. She really seemed to like Buster, and she liked to sketch him while he sat patiently waiting for Raymond to complete his laps. Raymond was familiar with the old routine of guys using their dogs to attract girls, but at first Buster was a little aloof when it came to Carol petting him. He hadn't really been exposed to the female of the human species.

Raymond always left Buster in their apartment when he went to class, but on this particular afternoon, Carol asked if Buster could join her by the pool.

Raymond was reluctant to release Buster to her care. He had come to enjoy Carol's company, and he was just on the verge of asking her out on a date, but he just didn't feel right about leaving Buster alone with her. Finally, he agreed, admitting to himself that he was actually a little jealous of anyone becoming involved in Buster's life.

Raymond left, reminding Carol that this was an afternoon when he would be home around five o'clock. He gave her a spare key to the apartment so if she grew tired of watching Buster, she could let him in and he would be all right.

He was home promptly at five, and he went directly to the swimming pool. He had a terrible sinking feeling in his stomach when he saw only an elderly couple in deck chairs reading the newspaper.

Raymond ran to their apartment, hoping to find Buster eagerly awaiting his return, perhaps just stretching and waking up from a nap on his favorite rug.

"But there was no Buster," Raymond said. "At first I panicked, then I took a deep breath, relaxed, and came to the obvious conclusion that Carol had taken Buster up to her apartment."

Raymond tried to calm himself, and he managed not to run up to Carol's apartment on the third floor.

"I did walk very quickly, though," he admitted, "and I probably pounded too loudly on her door so that I startled her neighbors."

A bleary-eyed man opened the door of the next apartment, scowled at Raymond, and grumbled that Carol always left for work around four o'clock.

Now Raymond was in a panic. Where was Buster?

No one seemed to know where Carol worked as a waitress, so Raymond was sitting on the stairs outside of her apartment when she came home a few minutes before midnight.

"I was in no mood to be polite, so I didn't apologize when she complained that I had startled her," Raymond recalled.

It had apparently been a hard night for Carol at the restaurant, for when Raymond asked the whereabouts of Buster, she shrugged and wondered how she should know.

"I left him in your care," Raymond said, trying his best not to raise his voice and awaken every occupant in the entire complex. "That is *how* you should know. What did you do with him? Where is he?"

Carol whined and leaned against her door. She was tired. Her feet were killing her. She'd had a hard night. "Let's at least go inside to talk so someone doesn't call security on us," she finally agreed.

She crossed the room and slumped down on a couch that was partially covered with sketches of Buster and some watercolors of scenic places. "I don't know where your darling little Buster is," she said around a yawn. "Ask the boys who took him to play with him."

What boys?

Exercising every ounce of patience and self-control he could muster, Raymond at last got the full story of what had occurred that afternoon.

A couple of young boys around twelve or thirteen years of age frequently came over from somewhere or other to hang out around the swimming pool. Although Carol knew they were not residents of the complex, she occasionally gave in to their pleas and opened the gate so they could swim in the pool. On this particular day, they were so taken with Buster that they begged her to let them take the cocker spaniel out of the pool area and play with him. Carol had said it was okay if they brought him back before five when his owner would return.

Raymond was furious. How could she let two complete strangers take Buster? He had entrusted his dog's safety to her.

Carol argued that the boys weren't complete strangers to her.

Well, then, Raymond demanded, what were their names so that he could go to their homes and retrieve Buster?

Carol narrowed her eyes, as if that would help her to remember. She mumbled that one of the boys was called Butch or Buddy and the other was named — she was almost certain — Jimmy.

And their last names were . . . ?

Carol responded to Raymond's demand

by admitting that she had no idea what their full names were. "But they *promised* to bring him back before five," she added self-righteously, as if their juvenile oath would absolve her from all guilt and responsibility for losing Buster.

Raymond headed directly for his car. He knew he would not be able to sleep with Buster lost somewhere on the streets of Costa Mesa. He desperately hoped that he might find him wandering, confused and frightened, somewhere near the complex where the two little dognappers had left him. Raymond drove until it was nearly sunrise, praying that he would see Buster just around the next turn.

"Ever since I got him as a puppy," Raymond told us, "Buster and I had never been separated for more than a few hours. The greatest fear that I had was that the boys would mistreat Buster. Or they might bring him home to parents who were too irresponsible to check Buster's dog tags and who would allow the boys to keep him. And then I would visualize some brutish father or older brother who might take delight in torturing little dogs."

After the horrible thoughts of someone abusing Buster were driven from his mind, Raymond would think of all the little bedtime rituals that the two of them had performed ever since Buster was just a tiny ball of fur. The loving pat on the head, the scratch behind the ear, the rubbing of the tummy, the little bowl of warm milk — Buster would receive none of those expressions of love that night.

And what would Buster be thinking? That Raymond didn't want him anymore? That he had been given away to these two kids who didn't know anything about the bedtime rituals or how he loved cream cheese on crackers? What had he done that was so terrible that Raymond would send him away?

Raymond skipped classes the next day to make up some posters and flyers with which he could blanket the several neighborhoods nearest the apartment complex. Surely, the two boys did not walk to the pool from miles away if they came there as often as Carol had said.

He staked himself out at the pool the next afternoon in the desperate hope that the boys might bring Buster back. Maybe they had responsible parents who would demand that they return a dog that quite obviously belonged to someone else.

But Raymond had no luck that day or the next or the one following. Carol broke her regular regimen of sunbathing and sketching and avoided the pool and Raymond.

Only once did he see her after Buster's disappearance. It was apparent that she had begun to feel at least somewhat guilty, but she again argued that the boys had promised to bring Buster back when they were finished playing with him. She really thought that they would do as they had promised.

Raymond forgave Carol for her irresponsibility, but he scratched all thoughts of a date with her. Her definition of a promise, a commitment to another, was too far distant from his own.

On the morning of Buster's sixth day missing, Raymond was awakened by the ringing of his doorbell. A neighbor in an apartment near his said that he must come to the pool at once.

There, standing at the gate of the pool area, he beheld the sight of his beloved Buster, but he was horrified to see that he was bleeding from several small wounds and that some of his hair had been pulled out in small clumps.

Buster began whining pitifully when he saw Raymond.

"It was then, as if realizing through his pain and disorientation that he had successfully managed to return to me, that Buster collapsed," Raymond said.

Raymond scooped up the cocker spaniel in his arms and asked the same caring neighbor if he would drive them to a veterinarian whose office Raymond had noticed was just a few blocks away. As he held Buster, Raymond was sickened to see several signs of abuse.

The veterinarian was startled and angered to see Buster's condition. From what he could ascertain, there were a number of welts and bruises on his body which indicated that the boys had tied Buster to a rope and used him for target practice with their BB guns. When Buster managed to free himself, he had probably been confused and had taken off running to get away from his cruel captors. There were also a number of bites and tears on the cocker spaniel's head and body that indicated encounters with much larger dogs. Buster had wandered the city for days until he managed to find his way back to Raymond.

After Buster's recovery, Raymond decided to move to another apartment complex. "Even though Buster recovered nicely from his terrible ordeal and wounds with my loving care, there were just too many bad memories at our former residence," he concluded. "I found another apartment just as nice and even closer to my college, so I would be away from Buster for even shorter periods of time."

CHAPTER 3
LEFT-BEHIND DOGS THAT FOUND THEIR WAY TO THEIR OWNERS' NEW HOMES

The mystery of how dogs can possibly find their way to homes where they have never lived, in places where they have never visited, seems an even greater mystery than dogs finding their way back to homes where they have previously resided. There have been a number of such ostensibly impossible classic cases recorded in the annals of canine enigmas, such as the following tales that we have collected over the past sixty years:

- Some Mysterious Force Guided Clementine from New York to a New Home in Colorado

  When Clementine's human family moved to Denver in 1949, she was left behind on the farm outside Dunkirk, New York, because she was about to become a mother. Three months later, her coat rough and matted, her paws cracked and worn, her bushy tail dwindled to a rag, she arrived at the front door of the family's new home in Denver.

How the loving and loyal Clementine had managed to negotiate rivers, mountains, and prairies to find her way to a strange house in a city where she had never been remains a mystery.

- Smokey Walked 417 Miles from Tulsa to Memphis

  In 1952, Smokey walked the 417 miles from the old homestead in Tulsa, Oklahoma, to the family's new place in Memphis, Tennessee.

- Chat Beau Traveled Three Hundred Miles from Louisiana to Find a New Home in Texas

  In 1953, Chat Beau took four months to hike the nearly three hundred miles between his owners' former home in Lafayette, Louisiana, and their new home in Texarkana, Texas.

- Pooh Hiked Two Hundred Miles from Georgia to South Carolina

  In less than four months in 1956, Pooh walked two hundred miles between his human family's former residence in Newnan, Georgia, and their new domicile in Wellford, South Carolina.

- **After Nearly Four Years, Another Smokey Found His Owners — After They Had Moved Twice**

  In the spring of 1966, a dog named Smokey (could it be something about the name?) found its owners, Mr. and Mrs. Phillip R. Bean of Seattle, after having been parted from them for three and a half years — and after the Beans had changed their place of residence twice.

- **Skippy Found a New Residence Six Hundred Miles Away**

  In his book *Strange World,* Frank Edwards wrote that in the 1960s, Skippy vanished from his home in Mount Clemens, Michigan, the apparent victim of a dognapper. Skippy returned to his astonished and delighted owner with a dog tag that had been issued in Fort Dodge, Iowa. Skippy had never been out of Mount Clemens before he went missing. How had he managed to find his way six hundred miles to his owners' new home?

MISSING FOR EIGHTEEN MONTHS, WHISPER FOUND HIS OWNERS IN THEIR NEW HOME

Scott Perry said the return of Whisper, their cocker spaniel, to their family was a true miracle. Whisper had been missing from the Perry family circle for eighteen months. But even more remarkable than Whisper's return on a summer day in 1995 was the fact that the cocker spaniel had disappeared when the Perrys lived in Freehold Township, New Jersey, thirteen miles away from their present home in Jackson Township. How had Whisper managed to find the Perrys in their new place of residence — and where had he been for those eighteen months?

At the time that Whisper vanished, the Perry family was desperate to find the dog who had become so very much an important part of their family. They put up reward flyers and posters on every pole and in every store window that gave them permission to do so for miles around their home. Many evenings after work, the whole family would get in the car to go searching for Whisper, hoping to catch sight of him wandering somewhere on a street, in a field, or in a park. They continued this practice for weeks without any success.

When the Perrys moved to Jackson Township, thirteen miles away, they sadly assumed that they would never see Whisper again. But one morning when Scott walked out of their apartment, he was astonished to see a cocker spaniel playing nearby with a group of children.

There was just something about the way the dog moved away from the children when they got a little too rough, something about the way he would give little yips and barks when he chased after the kids.

Very tentatively, Scott called out Whisper's name. At once, the dog's ears peaked and he turned his complete attention to the man who had said his name in that once so familiar voice. He left the children and came running to Scott Perry, whining as he rubbed up against his legs and jumped up and down for joy.

It was Whisper, appearing really none the worse for wear. As Scott called for the others to come outside to greet their long-lost friend, Whisper appeared very satisfied with himself that he had managed to find the Perrys in their new home.

Scott was exactly correct to call it a true miracle for the Perrys to have Whisper back in their family circle; however, there are questions that are likely to go forever unanswered. Why had Whisper wandered off from a family he loved so much, one that he cherished enough to find in their new home in an entirely new location a year and a half later? Had he been dognapped eighteen months before and had just managed to free himself? Did he return to the Perrys' former residence to find them no longer there? And if so, what manner of intelligence was at play that told him where the Perrys currently resided and how he could find their loving family circle once again?

LEFT BEHIND IN NEW YORK, OSCAR FOUND A NEW HOME IN INDIANA

The Hutchinsons experienced a canine miracle when Oscar, their beagle, traversed hundreds of miles to find them in their new home. When they moved from Niagara Falls, New York, to Indianapolis in October of 1988, the Hutchinsons decided to leave Oscar with a grandson who had always been fond of the dog.

Although Oscar must surely have understood that he would receive excellent care from his new owner, the beagle apparently just didn't feel comfortable in his new home — and it was very obvious that he missed the Hutchinsons terribly. His doggy mind may have understood that the Hutchinsons had the best of intentions when they decided not to subject him to the rigors of a move to a faraway, strange city, but, doggone it, they were his true family, and he belonged with them.

The fact that he had never before left the confines of the neighborhood in Niagara Falls didn't deter Oscar in the slightest and he set out in search of the Hutchinsons. Somehow, in some unfathomable way, he managed to arrive at their new home in Indianapolis seven months later.

It is quite certain that the beagle had no Rand McNally map tucked under his collar. We can't imagine that even if he had heard the street address of the Hutchinsons' new home repeated a hundred times before they'd left that Oscar could understand the concept of "Indianapolis" or how to find it. Yet, lean and bedraggled, his paws raw and bloody, Oscar arrived at the Hutchinsons' new home after an incredible seven-month trek.

Through the accomplishment of this seemingly impossible task, Oscar demonstrated in a most profound manner that he loved his old owners more than he esteemed the place where they had left him.

Even though the Hutchinsons had chosen to leave him behind, Oscar's unconditional love for them had managed to tap into a great mystery that provided him with the ability to find his beloved family in a distant city.

ROXANNA FOUND HER OWNERS IN A NEW RESIDENCE IN THEIR OLD HOMETOWN

Our friend Patty Ress, a reporter and author from Lincoln, Nebraska, told us that her parents often spoke of the little collie named Roxanna who returned after many years missing to find her owners in a new residence.

The McAllisters moved from Sioux City, Iowa, to a smaller town to raise their family. Of course, they brought Roxanna with them when they moved, and she adjusted nicely to the new environment.

After the McAllisters had been away from the city for several years, Roxanna disappeared. They could not accept that their beloved collie would leave them, and they suspected that she had been stolen by people passing through who wanted a nice collie. The McAllisters did all the usual things — put up posters, ran newspaper ads, and searched both the town streets and the country roads — but no Roxanna.

Mr. McAllister died, and about ten years after they had relocated to the small town, Mrs. McAllister decided to move back to Sioux City. With the children grown and time on her hands, Mrs. McAllister would work in the garden behind the duplex where she lived in retirement.

One day, while watering the flowers, she noticed a beautiful collie dog. She looked it over, and noticed that there was something terribly familiar about it.

She called out, "Roxanna? Is that you?"

Incredibly, after ten long years of separation, the dog wagged its tail and came running to Mrs. McAllister, licking her hands, face, and whimpering for joy. Several of the McAllister children came over that night, and Roxanna recognized all of them.

They could only guess where Roxanna had been during those ten years, but there she was again. The McAllister family theorized that after all those years, Roxanna had escaped from those who had dognapped her and returned to the McAllister home in the small town. Not finding the family there, Roxanna had set out for Sioux City, the place from which the McAllisters had moved.

Then, somehow, in that city of 85,000,

she had located the duplex where Mrs. McAllister was working in her garden. It need hardly be said that the two of them were never parted again.

HOW DO THEY DO IT?

The mystery of how a lost dog can find its way back to its owners after weeks, months, or years — and locate them in new and unfamiliar surroundings — may never be solved. Many explanations are given by self-proclaimed experts, but whether one argues for a group consciousness of all sentient creatures or guidance by angelic entities — or just dumb luck — no single explanation will satisfy everyone.

On some level of consciousness, all of us who love dogs and other animals have always known that there was a time in our ancient past when humans and animals enjoyed a much clearer communications link. In that less sophisticated era, devoid of science and technology, we humans had to rely on our keen senses and our own intuitive powers to stay alive. Furthermore, we knew that if we were to avoid becoming prey to the more powerful predators, we needed to become fast allies with certain of our animal cousins in order to survive the onslaughts of a deadly and hostile environment. Fortunately, the wolf — and its descendant, the dog — stood ready to evolve at our sides.

"Animals live in realms of their own, realms totally different and far older than ours," wrote Vincent and Margaret Gaddis in their book *The Strange World of Animals and Pets*. "They possess senses and extensions of senses that we have lost or never attained. They see sights we shall never see. They hear sounds we shall never hear. They respond to terrestrial and cosmic rhythms and cycles that we have never charted."

Dr. Larry Dossey, who served as a physician of internal medicine with the Dallas Diagnostic Association and as chief of staff of Medical City Dallas Hospital, has spent years of research exploring enigmas of mind and body, space and time, as well as the mystery of how animals find their way home against seemingly impossible conditions. Dr. Dossey suggests that one reason that we are so puzzled by accounts of lost dogs finding their way back to their owners quite likely lies in our assumption that the animal mind "is confined to its brain, and that it therefore cannot know 'at a distance.' Alternately, if the animal mind were not confined to points in space (its own brain and body) or time (the present moment), it (the lost animal) would be free to scan space and time and gain knowledge of 'the way home' over trails it never traveled before."

Dr. Dossey theorizes that humans and their dogs may possess a "non-local mind" which, with their individual minds, is part of "something larger that we cannot claim as our own private possession." In his thought-provoking book *Recovering the Soul: A Scientific and Spiritual Search,* Dr. Dossey explains how a study of shamanism and a review of the research conducted in telepathy presents possible explanations of how lost dogs many find their way home. Kinship with all creatures of the earth, sky, and water is an integral element in the practice of tribal medicine power. "If the record from shamanism is correct and meaningful interspecies communication does exist between humans and animals, then human knowledge of 'the way back' could conceivably be shared with the animal mind," Dr. Dossey says.

CHAPTER 4
THE WANDERERS
AND THE ROAMERS

In the stories in this chapter, the dogs were not dognapped, left behind accidentally while the family was moving, or chased off by unfriendly mutts during a vacation stop. These dogs quite likely wandered away from home when some member of the family inadvertently left a door ajar, a backyard gate open, or when the dog grew bored or curious and decided to go looking for adventure on its own. And then there is the reality that some dogs are born roamers and wanderers.

AFTER EIGHT YEARS, PETUNIA MADE IT HOME IN TIME FOR CHRISTMAS 2011

On a typical morning on the family farm near Fredericksburg, Virginia, in 2003, Kristen Pruitt let Petunia, their pit bull, outside with the other dogs to go about their morning wake-up duties. She saw Petunia run down toward the alpaca barns, which was her usual routine. When Kristen opened the door a few minutes later to let the dogs back inside for breakfast, Petunia was not among the others. The three-year-old pit bull had disappeared without a trace. And so she would remain until December 3, 2011, when the Pruitts received a telephone call informing them that Petunia had been found in rural Yuba County, California, three thousand miles away.

How Petunia arrived in the remote Spenceville Wildlife Area near Beale Air Force Base will quite likely forever remain a mystery to all but the pit bull herself. What strange detour had sent her from the alpaca barns on the Pruitts' Virginia farm to a wildlife refuge outside of Sacramento can only be left to the imagination.

Fortunately, Petunia had been found by the perfect person, Meg Eden, an Oregon dog trainer who had been hiking the Spenceville Wildlife Area. Although Petunia had no collar or dog tags, Ms. Eden thought the friendly dog was not a homeless stray. She took the pit bull to the Yuba County Animal Shelter, where Debra Luis, the supervisor, found the microchip that would put them in touch with a veterinary clinic in Fredricksburg.

The Pruitts admitted that if the call that Petunia had been found eight years and three thousand miles after she left their farm had come from a stranger, they might have thought someone was playing a rather cruel joke on them. But when the news was verified by their own veterinarian, they knew that the eight-year-old mystery of Petunia's disappearance had been at least partially answered by her discovery — however weird the situation may have seemed.

The Pruitts and their daughter, who was only three at the time of Petunia's vanishing, were reunited with their long-lost pit bull on December 10, 2011, on *Fox and Friends.* Gretchen Carlson hosted the very emotional reunion, and the Pruitts were able to thank Meg Eden, who after locating Petunia had accompanied her on the flight to New York City.

Perhaps there is a rather disappointingly ordinary explanation for the mystery of how Petunia got from rural Fredericksburg, Virginia, to the wildlife area in Yuba County, California. The Pruitts remembered Petunia as a friendly and gregarious pooch. They told Rob Parsons of the Yuba City *Appeal-Democrat* (December 3, 2011) that she just may have got into someone's truck and gone for a ride. Whether that initial hitch-hike got her all the way to California seems doubtful, however. Petunia quite likely had several rides and encountered a number of kind, temporary owners along the way.

Certain researchers have noted that some dogs are ingenious about ways to get aboard many forms of transport, and if they are desperate to get back home they may become fearless in jumping aboard anything that they may believe is headed toward their family. Dogs have been known to jump on trains, buses, and even balance on the top of fast-moving pickup trucks.

The Pruitts were just happy that their fears that somebody had picked Petunia up for some nefarious purpose had not been realized.

CORKY RETURNS AFTER FORTY-FOUR DAYS MISSING

Richard and Susan Strom own the Whitegate Inn and Abigail's Bed and Breakfast in Mendocino, California. On November 3, 2003, Richard was hiking with Corky, their Portuguese water dog, in Van Damme State Park, located three miles south of Mendocino on Highway 1, when Corky ran off the trail a short distance and just seemed to disappear.

When Richard returned with the startling

news that Corky had become lost about one mile from the trailhead at the Pygmy Forest parking area, the entire staff of Abigail's Bed and Breakfast and the Whitegate Inn went immediately to call and to search for the dog that they all loved so much.

Highway 1 runs through the park, separating the popular campground area from the Fern Canyon trailhead to the east, the beach and parking lot to the west. The park has ten miles of scenic trail on the Fern Canyon path that leads to Little River. The Pygmy Forest, near the spot where Corky seemed to have vanished, is an area where mature, cone-bearing cypress and pine trees eight feet tall stand next to ones six inches tall and growing.

After hours of searching, Richard, Susan, and all of their innkeepers and staff members were completely baffled by Corky's disappearance. It was so unlike the big dog to run off by himself, to say nothing of ignoring everyone's call to return.

For several days after Corky went missing, staff members would walk the park and the surrounding neighborhoods. They nailed or pasted hundreds of posters throughout all of Mendocino County.

Susan Strom later told how their innkeeper at Abigail's Bed and Breakfast even posted a picture of Corky on the window of her car with information about the missing dog. A truly dedicated dog lover, the innkeeper placed little signs around the bed-and-breakfast with prayers that loving spirits would guide Corky back home to all those who loved and missed him so very much.

To help gain even more feet on the ground to search for the missing dog, the Stroms' head housekeeper's daughter brought Corky's picture to school with her and put all the kids on the alert to help find him

November passed into December. The beginning of the month was filled with one rainy day after another, and the weather became very cold. Corky had been missing for thirty days, and the hopes that he was still alive were bumping up against the harsh reality that he may not be.

Every now and then, someone would come by with their claim that they had seen Corky on some trail or other while they were hiking the park. But then, to make matters even grimmer, old-timers in the region would somberly declare that if Corky had been lost in the forest that long, he had likely been eaten by a mountain lion.

With so many people searching for the missing Portuguese water dog, results were finally forthcoming, but it was most certainly not the news that the Stroms had been waiting to hear. Someone reported the body of a dead dog lying in the bushes just ten feet away from the parking lot at the Pygmy Forest trail. That was about one mile from the area where Richard had last seen Corky.

Susan freely admitted that she could not bear to accompany Richard to drive to the area to retrieve Corky's body. She stayed home and cried.

But when Richard returned, it was with the good news that the body of the unfortunate dog was not that of Corky.

Over forty days had now passed with no sign of Corky. The Stroms had spoken with the forestry crews, the firemen, the mushroom pickers, and every hiker who came by their inn or bed-and-breakfast. They had asked all the business owners in Mendocino, Little River, Fort Bragg, Albion, Boonville, and elsewhere to please keep Corky's posters up on their walls or windows.

After forty days of his being lost in the woods during the onset of winter, optimism was beginning to wane, and the Stroms doubted that they would ever see Corky again. How could any dog survive that long without food and shelter in the harsh, wintry rains and snows?

On the evening of December 16, a man sighted a thin, bedraggled dog crossing Little River Airport Road. Every alert person in the area had heard about the Stroms' missing dog, so the man called out Corky's name. The dog ran toward him, and when he opened the door, Corky jumped in the car.

Susan recalled that they were overwhelmed with joy and disbelief when the man rang the doorbell at the inn that night about 7:15 P.M. Corky rushed into their arms, and they embraced him; he was muddy, battered, and about half the size he was on the day that he'd vanished.

The veterinarian found that Corky had lost twenty-six pounds, nearly half of his former body weight, and now weighed a mere thirty-nine pounds. The fur that had once been a rich, silky brown was now a coarse gray, and it had thinned considerably. Corky had incurred numerous and large superficial wounds, and the veterinarian counted over three hundred ticks that were burrowing into his flesh. The good news was that he had sustained no major injuries.

After forty-four days in the woods, Corky had returned home.

In an article which she penned for the

Mendocino Beacon (March 16, 2006), Susan Strom wrote that Corky had become a celebrity about town. People who don't even know them come up to them and ask, "Is that Corky, the miracle dog?"

ROAMING IS IN SOME DOGS' GENES

Dr. Nicholas Dodman, founder of the Animal Behavior Clinic at Tufts University, reminds us that the living ancestor of the dog, the wolf, roams in order to survive and that roaming is a "natural behavior that involves scouting, hunting, exploration, and discovery." Home for the wolf, its den, is "reserved for family affairs, but all other good things in life are procured by skillful exploration of their home range," which may extend for many square miles. Nature has gifted the domestic descendants of those roaming wolves with a superior navigation system that enables them to create and store mental maps and, within reason, the wandering dog never gets lost.

In addition to neutering as a precaution against a wandering dog, Dr. Dodman, author of *If Only They Could Speak* (2002), recommends that caring dog owners erect a sturdy, solid fence to prevent both their own dogs from wandering away and to keep other people's dogs from unwanted visits.

Based on his research, Dr. Dodman cautions against runs, ties, and electric fences because they do not keep other dogs from intruding and they often increase territorial aggression in some dogs. Dr. Dodman also urges all dog owners to make the environment in which the dog is enclosed to be as canine friendly as possible, with proper attention to the pet's basic needs, especially a well-balanced and sensible diet.

TRY NOT TO TAKE IT PERSONALLY IF YOU HAVE A WANDERER

Although Brad (the co-author of this book) was only a young boy when he had a number of dogs that were the roaming kind, he still remembers suffering the typical reactions of anguish and self-recrimination experienced by those who have had a dog go missing.

When Brad was a boy on the farm, his father bent an ironclad rule of never owning more than one dog to help with the farm-work by getting a rat terrier puppy for his young son. Old Bill, their stalwart collie, their dependable canine "hired hand," sniffed Toby and seemed able to tolerate the puppy. Bill was probably counting on some help herding cattle, protecting the chickens, and guarding the small livestock from nocturnal raids by marauding packs of wild dogs, hungry skunks, raccoons, and foxes. Brad recalls how much he loved little Toby, how happy the puppy made him feel — and how desperately sorrowful he felt when Toby disappeared one night after only about a month of living on the farm.

Brad's parents said that Toby had simply wandered off. Brad should not take it personally. And they made certain that Brad did not consider that Toby might have met an unpleasant fate by encountering any of the midnight raiders mentioned in the above paragraph.

The next dog to replace Toby in Brad's affections was a puppy that stayed on the farm for so little time that Brad cannot even recall its name and remembers only that it had long ears. Brad's father explained that some dogs were just roamers by nature.

A husky, brown-and-white shepherd-mix pup arrived soon afterward, and it was now more important than ever that this dog stay put on the farm. Old Bill had crossed the Rainbow Bridge to Doggy Heaven, and the family badly needed another canine hired hand. Brad did his part by asking his grandmother, the town librarian, to help him pick out just the right name for his new dog. Grandma Dena suggested Rex, which means "king" in Latin. Rex it would be. A very suitable name for a dog that must perform many utilitarian tasks well, as well as being a companion for a boy and his little sister.

The months went by, and all seemed well with Rex. It appeared that he didn't have the roaming instinct and was content to stay on the farm and judiciously perform all the duties required of him.

Then, one afternoon, Rex didn't come home from the field where he had been chasing rabbits while Brad's father mowed hay. Brad prayed as hard as he could that God and the angels would bring Rex home.

Rex did return the next day, limping terribly and covered with blood. Apparently Dad had accidentally clipped one of Rex's hind legs with the mower. They took the injured dog to the veterinarian and nursed him back to health. But Rex had apparently had enough of the risks of farm life. As soon as he could walk reasonably well, he left the homestead after dark one night.

Brad felt that the family must be under a curse when it came to being able to keep a dog that was not a roamer. Why couldn't they get a dog that would be happy to stay with them?

At last, such a dog appeared and she made

her home with the family for over fifteen years. And a most unusual dog she was. Brad, his parents, and his little sister went into the woods where a farmer who supplemented his income by trapping said that there was a wild collie and her young pup. The pack had left the female behind when she was having pups, and she and the surviving pup — a white collie-who-knew-what mix — continued to live near the creek. The family managed to capture the pup and bring her home. They had to keep her penned up for weeks because she was so vicious, but when she finally decided to accept her human captors, she became the most devoted dog one could ever wish to acquire. Interestingly, she did all her chores on her terms. No one commanded the dog rightly named Queen; she did everything her own way. But her love, once it was won and deserved, was truly unconditional, even to the extent of single-handedly fighting off a pack of wild dogs that attacked Brad's mother one night when she was alone at home. The newly domesticated white collie had decided that she was not the roaming kind.

GYP, THE ROAMING DOG THAT LOVED CHRISTMAS

Brad may have had some difficult times with roaming and wandering dogs when he was a boy, but surely one of the most bizarre lost-and-found roaming dogs stories is the one that Allen Spraggett tells in his book *The Unexplained* about Gyp, a German police dog owned by Herbert Neff of Knoxville, Tennessee.

Neff got the dog in 1930, but Gyp kept running away from home. Strangely, he always returned to the Neff family at Christmas. Gyp would eat his fill of turkey with all the trimmings, then disappear for another year. The Neffs never had the slightest clue where the dog was for the other 364 days of the year, and they simply had to regard Gyp as their "Christmas dog," for he came back on each successive December 25 for nine consecutive years.

EDDIE FOUND HIS WAY HOME OVER FOUR HUNDRED MILES TO BE WITH JIMMY*

A marvelous resource for us as authors

* The names of the actual individuals in this account have been changed at their request to protect their anonymity.

always seeking new stories is The Steiger Questionnaire of Paranormal and Mystical Experiences (found on our Web site, www .bradandsherry.com). This questionnaire has been distributed by mail and e-mail since the late 1960s and has been returned by nearly forty thousand individuals from all over the world. Here is one of the stories gleaned from our questionnaire files.

Grant, an architect who lives in a suburb of Omaha, Nebraska, told us a touching story of his family's dog Eddie, a young beagle, that wandered off while they were visiting relatives and found his way back home after a journey of over four hundred miles.

In March 1996, their three-year-old son, Jimmy, had pedaled out in the street on his new tricycle and was struck by a neighbor coming home from work. Although the woman had already slowed her car as she approached her driveway, Jimmy was severely injured. He lay in a coma for a month, and Grant and his wife, Charlene, feared that they would lose him.

When Jimmy awakened, he had lost the hearing in his left ear and the sight in his right eye. In addition, he was paralyzed on his left side.

"Although it was difficult to remain optimistic about Jimmy's future at this point," Grant admitted in his correspondence to us, "our doctors were very positive. They pointed out that Jimmy was just a child and that the body can accomplish marvelous healings on its own. In time, his hearing could be restored. While he might never have full sight in his right eye, he could be fitted with glasses that could compensate a great deal for full vision. And the doctors were all extremely confident that in time, with physical therapy, Jimmy could recover most of his natural movement on his left side."

Grant told us that Charlene was "one of the original look on the bright side of life" girls, so one night when Jimmy was home from the hospital and lying quietly beside them on the couch, she suggested getting him a puppy. Charlene argued that they had to come up with something that would lift Jimmy's spirits and, at the same time, encourage him to move as much as possible. What better solution than a puppy?

Jimmy's fourth birthday was just days away, so right after cake and ice cream, Grant and Charlene introduced their son to a very energetic beagle puppy.

From the look on Jimmy's face, they had made an inspired choice. They were delighted to see that the puppy seemed to lift their son's spirits at once. Jimmy named his new friend Eddie, and they became inseparable companions.

Grant and Charlene were so pleased and greatly relieved that they had discovered an antidote to ward off Jimmy's loneliness. Eddie never left to go anywhere — except when Grant or Charlene carried him off Jimmy's bed for a potty break in a designated area.

As often as possible, Grant would place Jimmy in a stroller, tie Eddie behind it, and take the two for long walks around the neighborhood. Grant knew it was important that the puppy get some exercise and that Jimmy see more of the world than his bedroom.

In July 1997, the family drove across the state to visit Grant's parents on their farm near Scottsbluff, Nebraska, a distance of about 450 miles. Jimmy loved watching his grandfather feed the livestock and life in the country in general. Grandpa even took him for rides on his favorite horse, High Pockets, and Eddie would run alongside them, trying to keep up with the pace set by the quarter horse. Eddie appeared to enjoy life on the farm as much as the rest of the family. Grant decided to extend their visit from four or five days to nearly the entire two weeks of his vacation time.

It was on the day that Grant and Charlene had the car packed and were to travel home that Jimmy began to cry out that Eddie was missing. The entire family was stunned. Where had Eddie gone?

Everyone began calling his name. Grandpa searched the barn. Grandma looked all through the house. Grant checked High Pockets's stable. Charlene walked through the apple orchard. And Jimmy sat in the car, crying out for Eddie until he became hoarse.

Mysteriously, Eddie had disappeared.

The family found themselves gathering in a small cluster to discuss possibilities. Had Eddie seen a rabbit and run off, chasing the fleet bunny into an open field beyond earshot? Worse, had Eddie fallen into the old well? Grandpa checked it, and they were all relieved when his flashlight revealed no Eddie lying at the bottom.

They were all baffled, Grant recalled. "Eddie saw we were packing, and he loved to ride in the car. Why would he leave Jimmy's side? What had lured him away?"

It was finally time when they could put off leaving no longer. Grant had already told everyone that he must be in the office the next morning and they had a very long drive ahead of them.

Although Jimmy was already hoarse from calling Eddie's name, he cried for his lost friend all the way home, through the entire 450 miles. Over and over, Charlene and Grant kept telling him that Eddie would come back to Grandpa and Grandma and that they would bring him home.

The effects of losing Eddie proved devastating to Jimmy. He would not eat and he barely slept, sobbing in his bed, staring at Eddie's empty basket. It appeared that Jimmy had lost all interest in life.

As the months passed, Jimmy grew more listless and despondent. When they had first returned from the farm, Grant and Charlene knew that Jimmy had kept alive a hope that Eddie would return to his grandparents and that they, in turn, would bring his beloved friend back to him. Although Grant told us that they did their best to keep such a dream of a happy reunion alive, they knew that such a possibility became less likely as the weeks went by.

"It was heartbreaking to hear Jimmy say his prayers at night, asking God to bring Eddie back to him," Grant said. "Charlene would pray with him. We dared not think what would happen to Jimmy if all his hopes of ever seeing Eddie again were dashed."

Then, on November 8, Jimmy told his mother that he could hear something scratching at the front door. "It's Eddie," he exclaimed. "He's come home!"

Because Grant was still at work, Charlene was somewhat hesitant to open the door, but Jimmy kept insisting that Eddie had come home. When she opened the door, she was astonished to see a woefully bedraggled young beagle, whimpering, teetering on the doorstep.

Eddie limped to Jimmy's bed and tried to jump up beside him, but he was too weakened and disabled to manage. Weeping tears of joy, Jimmy leaned over and pulled Eddie up with his right arm. Although the beagle was filthy, Jimmy pressed Eddie to his side and hugged his battered little body.

"It had taken Eddie nearly four months to walk those 450 miles back home, but he had accomplished it," Grant said. "That little beagle had accomplished what had seemed an impossibility — to come back to Jimmy, the little boy who he loved so very much."

Grant rushed home in response to Charlene's telephone call announcing the miracle of Eddie's return. The power of prayer may have guided the tough little beagle home, Grant thought, but it would now take the power of veterinarian medicine to make him whole again.

After Eddie had a little something to eat and drink, Grant took him immediately to a veterinarian. Eddie had a number of infected areas that had to be treated at once. A portion of his left front paw would have to be amputated. The vet theorized that he may have been retrieving bait from a trap to get something to eat and the trap had sprung closed on his foot. Eddie had managed to pull free, but had left a portion of his paw behind.

A few weeks later, Eddie was pretty much restored to health, and the miracle of his return had inspired Jimmy to begin to walk on crutches.

No one would ever know why Eddie had suddenly wandered away. The most common theory was that something had frightened him and caused him to run a long distance. When he got near enough to the farm to see that his human family had left him, he ran away again, confused and bewildered as to why they had left him behind, but determined to find his way back home.

"If Eddie had not returned, Charlene and I dread to think what might have become of Jimmy," Grant said. "He had become so mired in despair over the loss of Eddie that he seemed to have lost the will to live."

Jimmy will always remain convinced that it was his prayers and tears that guided Eddie home, but he wishes over and over that Eddie could talk and tell him just what happened to him on that terrible day when the family had to leave him behind in the country.

LOST DOG STRUCK BY A CAR CHECKED ITSELF INTO A HOSPITAL

Fabian Ortega was beginning to wonder if he would ever see his dog Buddy again. Buddy was more than a friend to Ortega. According to the Long Beach *Press-Telegram* (October 4, 2006), Buddy was a trusted and faithful employee who had never missed a single day of work, nor had he ever even been a minute late for work.

Ortega owns a construction equipment rental business in Bellflower, California, and Buddy, his six-year-old German shepherd mix, was "chief of security," so Fabian was understandably worried when he realized his pal was nowhere to be found.

Ortega was having the fence around the site repaired, and it must have been during the patch-up process that Buddy found a way out of the yard. Ortega scoured the entire area for hours at a time, searching for

Buddy with no hint or clue as to where he could be. The days stretched into a week, then two weeks, without so much as a single clue as to Buddy's whereabouts. Ortega tried his best to remain hopeful, but by now he feared that something must have happened to Buddy and that he would never again see his faithful companion and guard dog.

Fabian Ortega had all but given up when he received a most welcome telephone call. Aaron Reyes identified himself over the phone as the director of operations of the Southeast Area Animal Control Authority (SEAACA), located in Downey. Reyes proceeded to tell Fabian that he was certain that his missing dog Buddy was there with him at the facility.

A strange twist of fate had intervened that would ultimately be one of the factors in favor of reuniting Buddy and Ortega. Five years earlier, Ortega had adopted Buddy from this same SEAACA facility, where it was procedural to implant a microchip for identification and tracking purposes. It was the very information contained in this chip that led to locating the dog's owner.

However, there was a more unusual element involved in how Buddy arrived at the SEAACA facility, and it was this part of the story that made local headlines.

It was apparent, Aaron Reyes said, that the dog had been hit by a car. He didn't know where that had occurred, nor did he know how this six-year-old German shepherd–mix dog knew how to find Kaiser Hospital in Bellflower and drag himself there *after* he'd had been hit by a car.

Reyes said it was a big mystery as to how Buddy ended up at the hospital. Hospital employees noticed the dog navigate his way through the automatic doors, as if he knew where he was going. He limped his way past the desk, heading straight to the emergency room.

A security officer was called to escort the dog out of the hospital, yet Buddy courageously and with determination managed to drag himself *back into* the hospital ER, and once again quietly lay back down in the waiting room.

Kaiser Hospital nurse Vangie Co'Vivo said it was apparent that the dog was not going to move until he was treated or seen by a doctor. No one was able to coax him into standing up. Even with the obvious pain of a dislocated or broken leg, the pooch showed no aggressive behavior, but in fact was very docile.

Nobody recognized the dog or knew him

to belong to any staff member of the hospital, so it was at that point that the decision was made to call the SEAACA to come and pick up the friendly pooch.

Employees at the hospital joked from that point on that as far as they knew, Buddy was the first *nonhuman* walk-in patient the hospital had taken in. Was it the smell of a hospital, the lure of ambulance sirens, or just a very intelligent dog who knew he would be treated kindly?

Needless to say, it was a happy reunion between Buddy Ortega and his faithful and smart employee Buddy. Dr. Brunskill, the veterinarian from the SEAACA facility who treated Buddy's fractured and dislocated leg, made the pronouncement that he was alert and in good spirits. Buddy, the German shepherd–mix wonder dog, was expected to make a full recovery and be back on the job at the construction equipment yard ASAP.

ZENA, THE WANDERING HUSKY, FOUND PEACE AT LAST

We first met Mary Beninghoff in the 1970s when she was a reporter for a major Indiana newspaper. Even as a busy journalist and book reviewer, she devoted every spare moment to animal causes. In her retirement years, she has volunteered her services full-time at animal-rescue shelters, currently at the Pet Refuge in Mishawaka, Indiana. Here, in her own words, is her love affair with Zena, a beautiful Alaskan malamute, who had a streak of wanderlust that made it difficult to remain in one place for very long:

I met Zena in 2003. She was one of the most beautiful creatures I'd ever seen. Her bright blue eyes could look through you, and if you passed her inspection, you had a good friend. It was love at first sight for me, but she took a bit longer.

Her hair was grayish with a soft ivory showing through, but it was her tail that held your attention. It flowed across her back and fanned out like a silver-gray rainbow. She was the epitome of what a malamute dog should be.

I was a volunteer at Pet Refuge in Mishawaka, Indiana, a no-kill cat and dog shelter. I'd lost my eighteen-year-old feline companion, Mahgy, the year before, and I had volunteered for about a year when I met Zena. I learned to love all the cats, but I had little contact with the dogs. I worked Fridays in the office and stayed after hours to spend time with the cats in the main cat room. Have you ever been totally covered with cats? There were at least forty cats free-roaming in the MCR and many of them used me for a bed while I sat there.

It was when I was working my day in the office that I met Zena. I had gone into the adoption area behind the office for a soda, and I heard a strange *Oooowww.* I looked around and was surprised to see a shadow inside the room that we called "the suite." It was a roomy area at the back of the building that had housed a dog that had been adopted several weeks before. I got closer and could see a dog standing there looking at me and producing another *Oooowww.* Her eyes clearly said, "Don't get too close."

I found her paperwork in the message bin and learned that she had been returned a few days before by her adopters: "Too much to handle." It was the second time for her to be returned since she was adopted as a puppy several years before. It was obvious by the notes on the adoption application that the interviewer had made it clear that she would be a very high-energy dog that needed to be walked frequently and liked to be outside with her human. The return form said, "Wanted to be let outside too much." Surprise! A malamute that wants to go outside often.

Zena and I developed our "eye" conversations over the next few Fridays and other days when I stopped by to sit with the cats. One day everything changed. Zena moved to sit at the gate to her suite and lowered her head as if she wanted me to touch it. For some reason I felt she wouldn't hurt me, so I went over to her and cautiously put a finger on her forehead, then two until my fingers were gently rubbing her. I swear she purred. It was the beginning of a beautiful friendship.

I always carried string cheese in my lunch on office days, and I started saving part of it for Zena. The first couple of times I held the whole piece of cheese, keeping my hands as far away from her teeth as I could. She would gently bite off a piece. After a few times I got brave and broke off a piece and held it out. She took it so gently that I didn't realize it was gone — and my fingers were intact and touching her teeth. We'd made another giant step.

During all this time I hadn't tried to go into her room. I asked our dog coordinator, Bonnie, if she would formally introduce us by going into the room with me. She did and I found myself standing a few feet from beautiful Zena.

She had a sofa, a chair, a TV, and a radio in her enclosure. Because I have a bad leg, I sat on the high sofa arm. Zena came over to me, put her head on my leg, and looked at me. This was our way of communicating from then on. If I hadn't had cats at the time (and Zena hated cats) I would have taken her home to foster.

Then the day came when Bonnie told me Zena had been adopted again. I was happy for Zena getting a home, but heartbroken because she was leaving. We said good-bye on Friday, and she spent some of the day with me in the office. I looped her leash onto a desk leg and she had ample room to move around, but she spent most of the time next to me with her head on my leg. Saturday, her new owner picked her up.

My Fridays were drab after that except for the time I spent with the cats. Then one day I came in, and Zena was in her room. I don't recall how long she was gone, but she got her fill of string cheese that day.

I was told that Zena had decided that she'd been gone from us long enough, and she had pushed open a patio door and was gone. Zena was on the run, and when we found her she was only a few blocks from the shelter. We could only assume that Zena was finding her way "home" and now she was back and we were all delighted.

Zena and I picked up where we left off. I thought how great it would be if my son could take Zena, but he had three dogs and the mix wouldn't work.

She was with us for quite a while again. We take back any of our pets that are returned for any reason, and if they aren't adopted again, we will keep them for life. Zena had a good life at the shelter so it wasn't too bad for her, but we had to remember, our goal was to find homes for all of our charges.

It wasn't too long before I heard that Zena had been adopted again. An older woman loved her looks and gentleness, and Zena had left the shelter once again. Unfortunately, against our advice, Zena was tied out on the woman's porch, and she slipped the leash. Her next adventure was about to begin.

Once we were told that she had run

away, our teams went out to the area to look for her. It shouldn't have been hard to spot a seventy-pound dog that looked like a wolf from a distance, but she eluded our searches. We put up posters in the area and then began to get phone calls that she had been seen heading north (the lady lived south of Pet Refuge), but again, she couldn't be found.

A few days later, only a few blocks from Pet Refuge, she stopped at a yard where a little girl was playing with her dog. The girl's father called Pet Refuge. I was in the office on a Friday and took the call. He said that he had found a gray dog and asked if we could take her in.

I explained that we couldn't take her, but I could check for a microchip, which many animals now have. An hour later, I let him and his daughter in with the dog following. Although her tail was scraggly and torn and she was dirty, I didn't need a scanner. I don't know who was more excited as we recognized each other. Zena was "home" again, and I hoped her adoption days were over. We never found out what happened to her gorgeous tail, but it didn't matter; she was back.

After an unofficial vote by our volunteers a few days later, it was decided Zena would stay with us and become our official mascot. She would not be adopted again and would be with us forever. Everyone celebrated by bringing her treats and fuzzy toys, and she and I settled into our routine again.

I spent a lot of time with her in her suite or in the office with her head on my knee "talking." It was great knowing Zena was back for good, and she seemed as happy as we were. But, alas, it was not to be.

Everything was going well, and Zena was all settled in until one day a volunteer arrived at Pet Refuge to begin her shift. She said the door opened too easily with her key, and it was cold in the room. Hoping the furnace had not failed in the night, she checked further and discovered that Zena's door was open both inside and out. Further checks showed that the lockbox where we put checks and cash had been forced open, and the office had been searched. Zena was nowhere to be found.

When the police arrived they took the report and said there was little hope of getting anything back. Checks would be thrown away and cash spent. And Zena was a missing dog.

Most of us knew Zena's talent for getting "almost home," but prayers were loud and frequent those days. We didn't know if she had wandered through the open gate or had been taken by those who broke in. Regardless, we wanted her back and the search began. Teams of our volunteers spent hours searching for her. There was no way of knowing which way she'd gone so the search was sporadic, at best.

Soon phone calls started again. "A big brown dog . . . ," "a wolflike dog . . . ," and my favorite, "a kinda friendly-looking dog with white hair." All were coming from the same area, and we searched there.

Finally, a call came from a woman who said her neighbor had found a large "Eskimo-like" dog and wanted to keep it.

Our coordinator, Bonnie, went to investigate. There Zena stood, flanked by two huskies. She hated other dogs, but two close to her own kind must have calmed her. She was less than a half mile or so from the shelter, heading in the right direction.

Again, Zena made it home. And there she stayed until the winter of 2009.

I had had cancer surgery in October of 2008 and because my knees locked up from inactivity, I couldn't go home on the day I was supposed to. I ended up in a nursing home in a wheelchair for therapy.

One day Bonnie and Molly from the dog department brought Zena to see me. Zena had been having problems with her hips, but she came over to me and sat down with her head in my lap. We sat that way a long time while we visited.

Zena had lain down after a while and had trouble getting up from the tile. Bonnie and Molly had to put a coat under her to help her rise. She was in pain, but I got a kiss from her. The last I would ever get from my beloved Zena.

One night, several weeks later, still at the nursing home, I dreamed of Zena. In the dream I was sitting on the side of my bed and Zena was in her familiar position, her head on my leg. We sat a while, in the dream, and then she rose, looked at me, and left. I woke with an aide asking why I was sitting up and crying. She said I told her, "Saying good-bye to a friend."

Later that morning, I got a call from Sandy, president of Pet Refuge. I said, "It's Zena, isn't it?" She said, "Yes, Zena went over the Rainbow Bridge last night."

I told Sandy about my dream and what had happened and she agreed Zena had come to say good-bye to me.

I think of Zena often. She had so much dignity and courage and love. She could have been lead dog on a sled team in Alaska, but she became a marvelous therapy dog. She often visited various nursing homes while she was with us, including with me, and she was so gentle. Zena spent her days surrounded by people who loved her. And still love her.

Bonnie took her home with her when it was apparent that she needed more care. Bonnie and Sandy were both with her when she left us. But in my mind she never left. She came to say goodbye to me, and I know Zena will always be with me and with those who loved her at Pet Refuge.

Zena never traveled the thousands of miles that some pets do to get home. Hers were short distances, but she knew where she wanted to be — and when she needed to, she somehow made it *almost home* so we would find her.

We'll never know how far she strayed on those unfortunate outings or what she experienced as she headed home, always in the right direction, so she could be found nearby, almost home. And we never found out what happened to her beautiful tail, but that didn't matter. Although we have had many memorable animals at Pet Refuge during my time there, Zena is still remembered. She was, and is, truly loved.

DOES YOUR WANDERING DOG HAVE A PHOBIA?

Some dogs are prone to be wanderers and roamers because they were born with a predisposition toward fearfulness or they developed a fear during their socialization process. Experts note that there is a fairly narrow window of opportunity for a puppy to be properly socialized. As young as eight weeks, a puppy may begin to show signs of extreme shyness or to exhibit fears of certain sounds, objects, or experiences. If these fearful responses are not dealt with at this time, by eight months, the puppy may have developed phobias prompted by loud noises, other dogs, or specific humans, such as young children or strange men and women.

Dr. Stanley Coren, author of such works as *How Dogs Think* and *Why We Love the Dogs We Do,* lists such signs that your dog is experiencing fear or anxiety as "flattened ears, tail lowered between the hind legs, cowering, slinking, yawning, hair raised on the back of the neck, trembling, drooling, or panting. The dog may also cling to the owner, whine and whimper, or even dribble puddles of urine. . . . The dog may show distressed behaviors, ranging from pacing and destructive chewing to growling or snapping at individuals who are the sources of its fear, or even at its owner or other family members."

Treatment for the fearful dog's phobic responses is difficult. Owners may have good intentions when they pet their dog or give it treats and gentle words, but such actions may only serve to reinforce the fear by indicating to the dog that the owner approves of its response to the phobia-inducing actions. The same rule that applies to reflexive human responses to a dog's fear is the same as not shouting at the dog when it does something the owner deems as wrong, such as chasing cars, cats, or neighbors. A human's shouts to a dog sound like barking, thus encouraging the dog to continue the wrongful action.

Dr. Coren advises that there now exists "a collection of veterinary pharmaceuticals to calm the dog and reduce its emotional state." However, if one is patient, "ignoring the dog's anxiety and going about things normally is often the best way to blast through the emotional problem." At first the dog may be puzzled by the fact that you are unruffled by the sound of thunder, for instance. Why is it that you do not recognize the urgency and the danger that he senses with the loud booms in the sky? Eventually, with your encouragement, if the phobia is not too deeply seated, your dog will decide that if you, as the leader of pack, are not frightened, then neither does he have any need to fear when the dark sky rumbles.

CHAPTER 5
ALONE AGAINST
THE WILDERNESS

NICK AND CHINOOK,
LONG-DISTANCE RUNNERS-UP
TO BOBBIE

If by traversing a total of three thousand miles, Bobbie the wonder collie of Oregon holds the gold medal in the Olympics of lost dogs returning home by land, then Nick the Alsatian has secured the silver medal at two thousand miles. Since there were no individuals who served as witnesses to Nick's struggles, no kind strangers who stepped forward to present their stories of her perseverance as there was in Bobbie's case, we have no way of knowing how many false starts and stops that she underwent before she reached Selah, Washington.

What we do know is that the courageous Nick, a five-year-old Alsatian female, became separated from Doug Simpson, her owner, while on a camping trip in the southern Arizona desert in 1979. Four months later, Nick struggled to find her way back to her home in Selah. Even if Nick had managed to travel a more or less straight line, that would mean that she walked over two thousand miles. Somehow, Nick managed to conquer some of the roughest country in North America, terrain that includes the Grand Canyon, a number of icy rivers, and the towering, snow-covered mountains of Nevada and Oregon.

Chinook, a white German shepherd, is the likely third-place winner for covering the greatest distance in a remarkable trek home. Chinook left Scottsbluff, Nebraska, in 1961 with his owner, Joe Martinez. Somehow, while staying in a Sacramento, California, motel, Chinook and Martinez became separated. Although Martinez spent hours searching for Chinook, he was forced to accept the sad fact that his dog had disappeared. In March 1964, Chinook limped, weary and ragged, into the yard of Martinez's former home in Scottsbluff. It had taken the shepherd three years to accomplish the 956-mile odyssey from Sacramento to Scottsbluff.

ANIKI RESCUED AFTER A MONTH ON MOUNT SEYMOUR

On June 30, 2007, Nam Hoang, an elementary schoolteacher, was hiking the area around Mount Seymour, British Columbia, with Aniki, a rottweiler cross, and Yuki, a Staffordshire terrier, when he became confused around Brockton Point and wandered east down a decommissioned ski trail into an area bordered by steep canyons, densely wooded terrain, thick brush, and waterfalls.

Hoang would later agree with search-and-rescue crews that there was no reason for anyone to go into that area. It would be so easy in the rough terrain to break a leg. Yes, Hoang would agree that there would no reason at all to enter what some called Indian Arm Canyon — unless one were lost and disoriented.

To add to the complications experienced by Hoang and his two canine companions, Aniki was struggling to keep up with the others because of the metal pin that had been placed in his left hip. The four-year-old rottweiler had been struck by an automobile, and Hoang had chosen to pay for an $11,000 operation for his beloved pet rather than put him down.

Hoang, thirty-five, was the recipient of a

lung transplant, and he was becoming concerned about his own medical condition at that altitude.

When the trio reached the top of a ridge, Aniki lay down, seemingly unable to go on. Although it was a difficult decision, Hoang left Aniki with assurances that he and Yuki would return for him. He told Aniki to lie still while the two of them continued down the slope and walked about three miles to Shone Creek.

The next day, Hoang asked two friends to go to the ridge and retrieve Aniki. The schoolteacher was grief-stricken when he was told that Aniki could not be found.

Immediately, Hoang contacted North Shore Search and Rescue for help, and they sent crews that spent three days searching for Aniki in the dense brush of the area. A helicopter refused payment from Hoang and flew over several locations on Mount Seymour, attempting to spot the lost dog.

Hoang went to the mountain every day at sunrise, before school began, and again at sunset, when the school day had ended, hoping that Aniki would detect his scent and follow his keen senses to his owner.

Hoang was moved by the fact that so many volunteers spent hundreds of hours searching for his Aniki. A Royal Canadian

Mounted Police dispatcher and her husband went out every day to look for the lost rottweiler.

The days turned into weeks. Hoang had begun to give up hope that Aniki would ever return to him after nearly a month had elapsed without a trace of his dear pet. If only his medical condition had permitted him to carry Aniki with him, rather than leaving the dog on that ridge.

Late on the afternoon of July 30, a female hiker approaching Brockton Point stopped to pet a very emaciated rottweiler. As she continued on her hike, she saw a maintenance worker and informed him about the dog that she had met on the trail. From her description, the maintenance worker was almost certain that she had encountered the dog that had been missing for a month. Immediately, he paged North Shore Search and Rescue.

As Tim Jones, the search-and-rescue coordinator, was headed up the mountain, he met a University of British Columbia professor of ophthalmology leading Aniki down with a rope.

Aniki had lost twenty-five pounds and had an eye infection, but a veterinarian determined that aside from near-starvation and the trouble with his eye, the rottweiler was in good condition.

Tim Jones said that from all the evidence that he could evaluate, Aniki had tried his absolute best to obey his owner's command to remain on the ridge where he had to be left. There was water nearby, and the rottweiler had likely foraged for shrubs and deer droppings to survive.

Jones also said that if Aniki had attempted to descend from the ridge with the handicap of his injured left hip, he would certainly have fallen down the cliff and been killed.

Hoang told journalist Kelly Sinoski that Aniki was doing very well, considering the ordeal that he had undergone during his four weeks on the mountain. In fact, Aniki, in spite of his weakened condition, appeared to be eager to be taken on walks.

IN SEVEN MONTHS, JAYNE CROSSED 650 MILES OF FORESTS, RIVERS, AND MOUNTAINS TO RETURN HOME

Jim Kreis of Hebron, Indiana, got a female beagle back in 1986, named her Jayne after a family friend, and raised her from a tiny pup on his farm outside of town.

In 1992, Jim got married, and after some time had passed, he was reluctantly forced to admit that the cozy little farmhouse that he had shared with Jayne was now just too small for the three of them. He could not bring himself to give Jayne away or to put her down, and he found himself in an emotional quandary. That was when his parents, Rick and Sharon Kreis, decided to help Jim out by letting Jayne stay at their place. Appreciative of their generosity and willingness to spare him the pain of getting rid of Jayne, Jim found time nearly every day to come over to his parents' home to exercise and to play with her.

In 1996, Rick and Sharon bought a saw-mill in Franklin, North Carolina, and moved away from Hebron, taking Jayne with them. On a brisk January day in 1997, Rick had let the beagle loose to chase after some rabbits. That was the last he saw of her.

The Kreises notified the local Humane Society and set out on their own search of the area around the sawmill. Sharon Kreis explained to journalist L. A. Justice in the *National Examiner* (August 19, 1997) that they had taken Jayne's Indiana dog tags off after their move and had been too busy to get her new North Carolina identification. The beagle — wherever she might be — would appear to be an unwanted stray, rather than the beloved member of a caring human family. Rick Kreis dreaded having to tell Jim that Jayne, his beloved beagle, had disappeared. What Rick and Sharon Kreis could not know was that Jayne had simply become homesick for her master, Jim, and the farm outside of Hebron, Indiana.

And although it took her seven months to find her way back home through unfamiliar territory, the sturdy little dog managed to accomplish her goal. She endured thunderstorms, heat, and freezing cold; she swam rivers and climbed mountains; but somehow the indomitable beagle walked the 650 miles from Franklin, North Carolina, to Hebron, Indiana.

On a warm summer day, a very roadweary Jayne staggered onto Jim's farmstead. She was painfully thin, and her paws were sore and bleeding. Somewhere along the route, she had lost a few teeth, but she was home.

Jim wasn't there to greet her, however. He had rented the house to a family friend, Paul Savage, and his girlfriend, Donna. As soon as they beheld the bedraggled beagle, they recognized her as Jayne, the one that was supposed to be living with Jim's folks in North Carolina.

Within minutes of receiving Paul's telephone call, a very surprised Jim Kreis roared onto the farm in his pickup. "I was absolutely amazed that she'd travel that far to come home," Kreis told L. A. Justice. "I guess that farm is the only home she knows."

Although he and his wife no longer lived on the farm, Jim said that Paul and Donna love Jayne and had agreed to provide her with a home. "I don't think she'll be running away again," he added.

TOSCA RETURNED HOME AFTER FIVE YEARS LOST IN A LAND OF TWENTY-THREE LAKES

New Brunswick's longest bridge harbors one of the most picturesque, historic sites from the shipbuilding era of days gone by. The Water Street Business District is home to a huge shipbuilding and timber/lumber enterprise established by the famed Cunard brothers. The Chatham Business District was officially designated New Brunswick's first provincial historic district under the Historic Sites Protection Act as recently as January of 2000. It is marked by a commemorative plaque which reads: "Historically, the Water Street area and the adjacent Miramichi riverfront bustled with shipping, shipbuilding, lumber industries and commerce. The enduring spatial quality and architectural character are reminiscent of the past." More then 450 ships were launched in Miramichi in its day.

The above provides a backdrop of what seems like an impossibly large area in which to find a lost puppy. So thought the Mac-Donald family when their beloved five-month-old black dachshund puppy, named Tosca, went missing from their home in Dartmouth, Nova Scotia, in October of the same year as the historic proclamation. Dartmouth, known as the City of Lakes, and which sports twenty-three lakes and a population of seventy thousand, is also famous for its year-round sporting activities, festivals, and world-class salmon angling, making the entire area a popular tourist location for many thousands to enjoy the culture, history, nature, beauty, and fun.

The MacDonalds had no idea how Tosca came to be missing, so their suspicion was that she had been stolen. Anyone could have spotted the adorable little dachshund and thought she would make a perfect gift or pet.

A dachshund just happens to have a temperament that is curious, bold, and always up for adventure. On the other hand, another characteristic of a dachshund is one of being reserved and suspicious of strangers, so perhaps Tosca broke away from her captor and could be wandering the area —

hopelessly lost. In any event, the Mac-Donalds wondered how it would be possible to find such a tiny puppy in a huge area with twenty-three lakes, vast woods, and tourist attractions covering a great expanse of land. Sylvia MacDonald, the dog's owner, was heartbroken and cried all night long, thinking she would never see her dog again.

The MacDonald family immediately went to work putting up posters in as many highly visible areas as possible in hopes that someone might recognize the missing dog and be of assistance in locating her. Indeed, the posters led to the first possible clue. The MacDonalds learned from a number of individuals that a woman in a nearby neighborhood had been seen with a similar-looking dog around the same time Tosca went missing.

Unable to locate the woman, her whereabouts, or any further information about her, the MacDonalds hired a private detective to assist in finding her and hopefully their Tosca. A dog resembling the black dachshund was in the possession of this woman at her home when the detective made contact, but she insisted it wasn't the same animal, and the detective did not see certain identifying characteristics unique to the missing Tosca.

The police were contacted to investigate further, but in the interim this woman moved to New Brunswick and was unable to be found. The family refused to give up their search for their cherished pet . . . contacting relatives and everyone possible to aid them in their search.

In the meantime, much time had passed without any further clue as to Tosca's whereabouts, but the MacDonalds were about to assign a new historic claim to Miramichi for something other than the shipping and timber industry, and that would be their own personal miracle. On a very ordinary day, five years later, the Mac-Donalds received a phone call that their missing dog just might have been found. Yes, that is *five years* later!

While driving on New Brunswick Highway 11, Kevin Burchill spotted a small dog just sitting by the side of the road. He was often accustomed to noticing stray dogs on that road, but in this case, the dog seemed to be lost and confused. To Burchill, it almost appeared that the dog was begging. He stopped and was able to approach the dog and notice it was wearing a rabies tag that had a phone number of a Nova Scotia veterinarian. Burchill called the vet and was given MacDonald's phone number.

Burchill dialed the number, described the dog, where he found her, and then was stunned to be told how long ago the Mac-Donalds' dog went missing. In fact, the initial reaction was that it couldn't be the same dog, but it did not deter the "what if it is?" possibility, and the MacDonalds called Kevin Burchill several times that same night and asked for more details.

It was the third phone call when Burchill vividly described two blond dots on the dog's eyebrows that sealed the hope that it could be Tosca.

The next day, Sylvia MacDonald and her husband drove to New Brunswick, where they were at last reunited with their missing Tosca — after five years! The MacDonalds claimed that her face had not changed a bit in all that time as they eagerly swept the dog into their arms and gave her a kiss. Tom Peters of the *Halifax Herald Limited* (July 25, 2005) wrote that the happy ending to the saga of Tosca reunited the dachshund with her sister dachshund and three other dogs — once again in their family home in Dart-mouth.

ORLI SURVIVED A CAR CRASH
AND THREE WEEKS IN THE
MOJAVE DESERT

On March 16, 2005, Ronnie Phillips was driving northeast on I-15 toward her home in Las Vegas accompanied by her golden retriever, Remington, and her black Lab, Orli. She was enjoying the scenic drive out of Barstow in the high Mojave Desert country of eastern California when she felt a bump, swerved to avoid what she believed to be something in the road, overcorrected, and lost control of her Saturn SUV. The vehicle smashed through a guardrail and rolled over.

Ronnie Phillips lay inside her SUV with a broken pelvis until the rescue unit summoned by the California Highway Patrol managed to remove her from the crushed Saturn. Once free of the collapsed vehicle, she was airlifted by helicopter to a hospital in Colton.

Once she was out of surgery and had regained consciousness, Ronnie's immediate concern was for Remington and Orli. She learned that a dutiful Highway Patrol officer had brought Remington to the Barstow Humane Society for care until a family member reclaimed him. She was assured that the big golden retriever had miraculously incurred no injuries.

But what about Orli, her black Lab?

No one seemed to know anything about another dog having been in the SUV with Phillips.

Once they received notice of a female Labrador having been involved in the crash, the Highway Patrol searched the immediate area, but were sorry to report no sightings of Orli. The tow truck driver who had been sent to retrieve the mangled SUV had taken time to search for the missing dog. Mrs. Phillips's daughter drove to Barstow and searched for quite a distance along Interstate 15.

Although so many people were sympathetic to Ronnie Phillips's concern for her missing dog, no one knew what might have happened to Orli. She may have been injured in the crash and managed to drag herself into the underbrush before dying or she may have wandered off in a dazed condition and been eaten by coyotes. After a week had passed without a single sighting of Orli, Mrs. Phillips accepted the inevitable: Orli had been severely injured and had crawled off to die. The predators and scavengers of the area would soon have made short work of the body and left few traces of her final resting place.

About three weeks after the crash, John and Denise Vissat of San Diego were driving their Jeep on a trail through the Mojave Desert between Needles and Barstow. Needles is located on the Colorado River just across the bridge from Arizona and the tip of Nevada, and Barstow sits at the junction of Interstate 15, Interstate 40, and State Highway 58.

It was a rainy, muddy day, and for some unknown reason (which John Vissat later viewed as fate), they decided to take a different route in the hope that they might find less soggy terrain. They had not driven far on the new trail when they spotted a black Lab with almost totally mud-caked fur. The Vissats knew that the animal was not a stray or a homeless dog because it had a collar and was dragging a leather leash.

The Vissats gave the emaciated-looking Lab some food and water, then John rubbed the mud off her tags and found a phone number and an indication that Orli bore a microchip ID.

On a Sunday evening, nearly three weeks after the crash, Ronnie Phillips, recuperating at her son's home, received a telephone call that the Vissats had found her beloved Orli. When she was informed that Orli was doing fine, she told columnist Diane Bell of the *San Diego Union-Tribune* (April 5, 2005) that it was "unbelievable, a miracle."

Ronnie Phillips's son drove to San Diego the next day to retrieve Orli from the Vissats. The black Lab was about twelve pounds thinner, but seemingly none the worse for three weeks of wear and tear in the Mojave wilderness.

BULL TERRIER ALIVE
AFTER TWO WEEKS OF CLINGING
TO A LEDGE ONE HUNDRED FEET
ABOVE THE OCEAN

In March 2007, while Margie Brett and her family were on holiday in North Devon in southwest England, Bush, their female Staffordshire bull terrier, disappeared. Immediately, the Bretts plastered the area with posters and involved as many residents as they could in a desperate search campaign.

Margie and her husband, Hugh, knew that Bush had last been seen as she was walking free of her leash near the cliffs at Combe Martin, Ilfracombe, but then it appeared that she had completely disappeared. Reluctantly, after several days, the Bretts had to return to Oxfordshire, where Margie was a magazine editor.

Two weeks after they returned, Margie Brett heard a news report telling of two climbers who thought they had spotted a dog on a ledge about a hundred feet above the sea. Brett immediately contacted the Coast Guard, and they relayed her message to a nearby Royal Air Force base. Fortunately, her request was heard by sympathetic ears. Brett theorized that her bull terrier might have been chasing an animal, perhaps a deer, that had veered away from the cliffs at the proper moment to continue its run but to trick Bush into plunging to the sea several hundred feet below. Rallying to her call for help, the RAF carried out Operation Dog Rescue as a training exercise.

When they got to the spot on the cliffs where the climbers had claimed to have seen a dog lying on a ledge, an RAF sergeant was lowered two hundred feet down the side of a cliff to reach Bush, who was in very bad shape. The sergeant called up that he had found the missing bull terrier, but she was so thin her ribs were sticking out.

How had Bush managed to stay alive for two weeks on a slender ledge a hundred feet above the sea?

The sergeant spotted a pile of crow's feathers next to Bush on the ledge. Somehow, the bull terrier had managed to grab a curious crow that had perhaps misjudged Bush as carrion and a snack of its own. In addition to the rather sparse flesh under all those feathers, Bush had been near enough to a waterfall to drink from the water running past her.

Margie Brett was quoted as saying in the *Daily Mail* (May 10, 2007) that she had never given up hope that she would once again hold Bush in her arms. That moment, she acknowledged, would occur just as soon as Bush was released from the veterinary clinic, where she underwent immediate care.

DON'T TAKE YOUR DOG OFF ITS LEASH IN STRANGE TERRAIN: MARTY SURVIVES BEARS, COUGARS, AND COYOTES — OH, MY!

Great true accounts on a variety of subjects come to us sometimes when we least expect them, such as the great experience that Phil shared with us after we had struck up an acquaintance with him and his wife in the Angry Trout, one of our favorite restaurants in Grand Marais, Minnesota.

Phil said that he will always remember the valuable lesson that he learned about an owner's responsibility to his dog when he was fifteen years old and on a family vacation to northern Minnesota in the summer of 1991.

Phil recalled that there seemed to be a

strange cloud of foreboding over the trip almost before it really got started. His father and mother, Ray and Donna, were in the front seat of the station wagon, and Phil and his eleven-year-old sister, Christi, were jammed in the backseat with Marty, their German shepherd, when the motor of the wagon emitted a terrible squalling, rasping screech, like the death cry of a metallic dragon.

Fortunately, they were not far from a gas station near the St. Paul/Minneapolis airport, so Phil's father managed somehow to maneuver their station wagon out of the traffic flow.

Everyone's heart sank, Phil said. The family figured vacation was over before they were even a hundred miles away from home. He remembered that Christi started to cry, and it looked like his mom wasn't far from tears. They had rented a cabin on Lake Superior, just a few miles from the Canadian border, and the family friends who had recommended the place never seemed to stop talking about how beautiful it was up in that far-north country.

Phil's dad was not to be bested by a station wagon in desperate need of repair. He filled out some forms for the manager of the service station, told him that they would be back in a week, and rushed the family out of the wagon and into a cab. They would rent a car and drive the remaining 250 miles to the resort.

Phil recalled that they drove away from a rental agency near the airport in a snug four-door that really crowded the kids and Marty in the backseat. The trunk was packed with his father's usual care and precision, so tightly that the proverbial mouse could not squeeze in between the suitcases.

They arrived at the resort just as a breathtakingly beautiful sunset was coloring the sky over Lake Superior. His father picked up the key to their cabin, and they drove on a lane that was barely distinguishable from the forest surrounding it. It was early in the season, and the grass and weeds growing in the lane had not yet been beaten down and dried by automobile tires and sun.

"It felt so good to finally get out of the car and stretch our legs," Phil told us. "Marty's paws scratched Christi's knee as he scrambled to free himself from the backseat and to relieve himself on a nearby bush."

And that was when Phil committed the unpardonable sin.

He had a grip on Marty's leash while the big German shepherd was obeying nature's call when he spotted a big jackrabbit crouching next to a birch tree.

"You have to understand," Phil explained to us, "I had grown up watching television reruns of *Rin Tin Tin,* the super German shepherd, *Lassie,* the invincible collie, and *Sergeant Preston of the Yukon* with the indomitable husky, Yukon King. Rusty never had Rinny on a leash. Timmy let Lassie wander all over the place. And even Sergeant Preston wouldn't dare to wrap a leash around Yukon King's neck, so I unhooked the leash from Marty's collar and told him to go get the jackrabbit."

With a roar that Phil thought was totally primeval, Marty took off after the jackrabbit.

Ray came out of the cabin and reminded Phil that there were more suitcases to carry inside. When he saw Marty's leash in Phil's hand, he yelled even louder than he did when the station wagon broke down in Minneapolis: "Where is Marty?"

Phil risked a casual bravado when he told his father that he had set him after a jackrabbit.

Phil said that he would always remember the look in his father's eye. His mouth opened and closed a couple of times, but no sound came out. When he managed to find his voice again, his words were almost a solid stream of anger and incredulity. He reminded Phil that Marty was a city dog who had never seen a jackrabbit. He had never been in the woods — and certainly not the thick forests of northern Minnesota. There were cougars, bears, coyotes, and wolves out there that could make short work of Marty.

Phil said he tried a couple of "C'mon, Dad — bears, wolves?" But he remembered that his father looked at him as if he were rearing a total moron.

Yes, his father told him, there were black bears in those woods. There were also cougars, mountain lions, panthers — call them what you will.

Phil fared no better when his mother and sister emerged from the cabin to see what all the yelling was about. When his father told them of the enormity of Phil's crime, his mother looked at him in disbelief and Christi began to cry and call him all the worst names she knew, such as "dumbhead" and "jerk."

Phil tried to downplay his misdeed, assuring them that Marty would be right back.

"So where was he?" his father countered.

Christi supplied the answer, shouting around tearful gasps that Marty was never coming back because a bear would eat him.

Phil admitted to us that an hour after Marty had disappeared in pursuit of the jackrabbit, he was becoming less confident in his decision to remove Marty's leash. He began calling for the dog, but there was no answering bark or reassuring surge of a big German shepherd through the bushes.

Phil got a flashlight from his backpack and told the family that he was going looking for Marty.

His father had cooled down a bit, so he told Phil that as much as they all loved Marty, the family loved their son more. It was now almost completely dark. It would probably take Phil less than an hour before he would be walking in circles and become lost. At least Marty had a super sense of smell that would help him find his way back to the cabin.

The family had eaten at a very nice restaurant in a small town near the resort. They would go into the village the next day and buy some groceries. Since it had been an exhausting day and an emotional one, Phil's mother suggested that they all try to get some rest and go to bed early. Marty would probably be scratching at the door by first light.

Phil remembered that he lay awake the

entire night, only fitfully drifting off to sleep for brief moments before he would awaken, stricken with grief for his stupidity and with fear for Marty out there alone in the forest. With the bears. The wolves. The coyotes. And the mountain lions. He kept trying to tell himself that his father was only exaggerating the dangers of the northern woods to drive home the error of his releasing Marty from the leash.

The next morning brought a raccoon scratching at their cabin door, but no sign of Marty.

A bit before noon, they drove into the village to pick up some groceries. Phil spotted a small police station and told his father that he was going to report that Marty was missing.

Phil said that the look on his father's face should have warned him that he was about to receive another valuable life lesson.

The older officer in the station listened quietly to Phil's description of Marty, and then asked if the dog was wearing his tags and how long the dog had been missing.

The younger officer, who appeared to be only a few years older than Phil, laughed out loud when Phil said that Marty had been missing since last night. He put down his newspaper and told Phil that he had better accept the harsh reality that he would never see his dog again. A city-bred dog would just be a snack for some hungry critter.

Phil protested, "But what if Marty found some farmers or came up to someone's house?"

The young officer shook his head in disbelief and told Phil that if any farmer who kept cattle or sheep saw a German shepherd prowling around on his own at night, they would take him out with a couple .30-30 slugs before they would check to see if he were wearing tags.

Phil had had enough. He left the small police station and joined his family at a nice rustic restaurant. He didn't feel very hungry. His visit to the local constabulary had put him pretty much into a downer.

At the table across from them sat three men and a woman who were speaking rather animatedly about their time in the northern woods. Phil didn't intend to eavesdrop, but the group had raised their voices in their conversation so that it was impossible not to hear most of what they were saying.

They were apparently all faculty members at an area college. The woman and one of the men were obviously biologists or zoologists, and they were talking excitedly about some wildlife sightings that they had made. The woman said that she had seen a large black bear shortly after they had arrived. One of the men, who somehow gave off the vibes to Phil of being a music professor, said that he would like to see a black bear and to pet its thick fur.

Phil recalled how the others had teased him for his naiveté and told him that the bear would rip off his arm if he tried to pet it.

The man who was apparently a zoologist said that he had been driving home two nights ago and had caught a very large cougar in his headlights.

Again, the music professor said that he would like very much to see such a magnificent cougar and pet it.

The others laughed and told their friend that he had seen too many Disney nature movies. "These aren't Bambi and Thumper out there," the woman chuckled. "These are real animals. They are wild animals. They are not domesticated pets. Why, they actually hunt dogs and cats at the local farms."

Phil told us that when he looked at the hamburger on his plate he knew that he had to get out of there or he was going to be sick all over the table — and his family. Because of his stupidity, poor Marty had probably been chewed to pieces by a cougar.

All Phil could think of on the long drive back to the cabin area of the resort was how Marty might have perished. Terrible images kept coming to his mind. Marty was a strong German shepherd, but he was just one dog against a whole forest of savage animals.

Several turns on the road back to the resort took their vehicle near trees and brush, and Phil would look desperately down every bit of clearing to see if he could spot Marty. Phil remembered that he kept telling himself that it might not be too late. Maybe Marty was somehow managing to avoid the bears, coyotes, wolves, and mountain lions.

That evening toward twilight, Christi and Phil were sitting on a wooden bench on the front porch when a small miracle occurred. A white-haired man approached their cabin, followed by Marty squeezing around his legs. Christi and Phil raced to hug and pet their beloved pet, shouting for their parents to join them in the celebration.

Scott, an eighty-year-old summer resident of the area, had been up late reading the previous night when he spotted an unfamiliar German shepherd prowling around the grounds after midnight. Knowing the danger the dog might face if he were left on his own during the night, he called to him and the dog came to him at once.

The next day, Scott cleaned off the tags around the dog's neck and discovered that Marty was from a town in Minnesota. Scott checked the license plates of all the cars parked at the cabins near his and saw that they were all from out of state, including the South Dakota plates on the rental car that the family had picked up in Minneapolis.

Scott sheltered Marty for the night, then the next morning went to check the guest registry at the office. When he saw that the South Dakota automobile was a rental to a family residing in the same Minnesota town as the one inscribed on Marty's tags, he brought him immediately to their cabin.

By the time that Scott got to the cabin, Phil and the family were off to the village, where they spent several hours. Scott brought Marty over to the family as soon as he finished his afternoon nap.

Phil said that the remaining days of their vacation were extremely enjoyable. "And I learned a valuable lesson," he told us, concluding his story. "If you care about your pet, you will take care of it — and not take it off its leash and allow it to run free in unfamiliar territory where it may easily get injured or lost."

CHAPTER 6
DOG OVERBOARD!

**DOG OVERBOARD! LOLA SWIMS
MILES BACK TO SHORE**

It was Friday, December 30, 2011. The weather and the sea were calm, the New Year was about to be born with new opportunities, and Mike Peters of Pompano Beach, Florida, was enjoying the afternoon with his girlfriend, Heather Wolfe, and another friend. Lola, Peters's four-year-old corgi mix, was sleeping contentedly.

Then, as they were returning their twenty-two-foot boat to the Hillsboro Inlet, Lola, who was between Peters's legs, suddenly fell overboard. Peters and the others desperately tried to sight her, but she was missing at sea. Lola was gone.

When they got back to shore, they began posting flyers about their Lola's disappearance in public places and also posted her picture on Facebook.

Lola normally wore a dog tag, but on this

particular day, unfortunately, it wasn't on during their boat trip. However, people would be able to recognize her easily from her picture. A few days before they went boating, a groomer had confused instructions and had given Lola a "lion cut" that had completely shaved her body hair, leaving only a mane on her head and shoulders.

Peters and Wolfe resolved to be optimistic about her fate. Lola was comfortable in the water. It was part of her daily routine to swim across the lake near their home. However, a small lake was not the ocean.

The fact that there were a lot of boats that day in South Florida also gave them hope that Lola would be spotted swimming in the water. It was a very calm day, and boaters could see objects in the water very clearly. Someone just had to have picked Lola up in their boat.

No one will ever know how many miles the corgi swam, but on Saturday a beachgoer found her wandering outside a Boca Raton hotel near the Intracoastal, a distance of over ten miles from the spot where Lola had fallen into the ocean. The beachgoer alerted the police, and at about 7:00 P.M., they called Ed Hubbard, a volunteer at the Tri-County Humane Society of Boca Raton. Once Hubbard got a leash around

Lola, he took her home with him.

Not knowing that Lola had reached land in Boca Raton, Wolfe and Peters were praying that there was a chance that Lola would be picked up by boaters or would be able to swim to shore. At this point, they had no way of knowing how many miles of sea Lola had had to conquer before she'd found land.

Hubbard tended to Lola over the weekend, and on Tuesday, January 3, someone saw an article on the missing dog in the South Florida *Sun Sentinel* and alerted him that he had Lola in his care. Hubbard then called Peters, who, according to Juan Ortega of the *Sun Sentinel,* was "tickled pink" that his beloved corgi had been found safe and in excellent condition. Happily, Peters and Wolfe would be able to face the new year with Lola, whom they proclaimed their "miracle dog."

TODD, A BLACK LAB, SWIMS TEN MILES OF STORMY SEA TO FIND HIS OWNER ONSHORE

On July 24, 2002, Peter Loizou was running his yacht against heavy winds as he approached the coast of the Isle of Wight. On board with Peter was Todd, his two-year-old black Labrador retriever, a dog that he held so dear that many of his friends had heard him declare that Todd was like a son to him.

Taking the briefest of respites from battling the winds, Loizou called for Todd, puzzled that the Lab was not at his side as he had been minutes before the winds and currents had become so strong. After a few desperate minutes, Loizou realized that Todd was missing. Somehow, perhaps when the yacht lurched against the windswept ocean, he was thrown overboard.

Loizou was now only about a mile off the coast of the Isle of Wight. He put in a call to the harbormaster, who promised a search of the waters crashing toward shore.

For four hours, Loizou frantically searched the area, shouting Todd's name even though he knew his desperate calls were taken quickly by the wind. He became despondent. After such a length of time, he knew that Todd, powerful swimmer that he was, could not successfully fight the winds and the strong ocean current.

Angrily, Peter Loizou swore that he would put the yacht up for sale. He never wanted to set foot on its deck again. The boat and the merciless sea had robbed him of his beloved Todd.

Later that evening, while Peter sat grief-stricken in his home in Winsor, Southampton, the shrill ringing of the telephone shook him from his silent misery. In astonishment, he found himself speaking with a police officer who presented him with the incredible news that they had Todd with them at the station. A teenage boy had brought him in to the authorities. The microchip in Todd's ear had identified the black Lab and provided all the necessary data to reunite him with his owner.

Later, Peter and the police reconstructed Todd's nautical adventure. Although the Lab was only about a mile from the coast of the Isle of Wight, the dog apparently wanted nothing to do with that place; he wanted to go home.

Guided by some marvelous internal compass, Todd headed instead for the Solent Waterway and the English mainland. Indeed, it would have been easier to swim that one mile to the Isle of Wight, but Todd courageously charted a course through the longer route across the Solent, through busy shipping lanes, and against heavy offshore winds that could well have blown him in the opposite direction.

After he had swum about five miles, the navigational impulse guiding him told him to alter course and head up the River Beaulieu for his home in Winsor.

Six hours and ten miles after his ordeal by

sea began, Todd pulled himself onto dry land just a few miles from the house where he knew he would be reunited with Peter. Exhausted, but game to struggle on the rest of the way home, the Southampton *Daily Echo* (July 24, 2002) reported, Todd was picked up by the compassionate sixteen-year-old boy who brought Todd to the authorities.

Although Labradors are known to be great water dogs, Peter resolved never to put Todd to such a test again. Todd swam ten miles across windswept waves and powerful currents to get home. Such a feat proved his love, strength, and endurance for a lifetime.

MOLLY, SOLE SURVIVOR OF A BOATING ACCIDENT IN THE ALLAGASH WILDERNESS WATERWAY

When Doug Harmon of Scarborough, Maine, entered the Allagash Wilderness Waterway with his black Labrador, Molly, he was looking forward to a pleasant Memorial Day outing on Chamberlain Lake. Molly had been the first dog that Harmon had ever owned as an adult, and the two were inseparable. Harmon's kids, Jared, fourteen, Timothy, twelve, and Ashley, eight, may have felt a trifle jealous at not being invited for the trip over Memorial Day

171

2007, but they respected their father's right to have a little time to himself.

But the boating trip ended in tragedy. Joan Pelletier, the children's mother and Harmon's former wife, had to break the news that their father and another man had drowned when their boat capsized after being caught by high winds on Chamberlain Lake.

Dealing with such enormous grief is difficult at any age, but the death of one's father is especially problematic for the mind of a young child to comprehend. Little Ashley, knowing how close her dad and Molly were, sobbed and said that she and her brothers would have to take care of Molly for Daddy.

After that tearful declaration, Ms. Pelletier had no choice other than to inform the children that Molly, too, had drowned in the lake.

But men at the accident scene told Harmon's brother, Greg, that they had not discovered the Labrador's body and that one of the investigators was certain that he had found a set of paw prints at the shore.

Department of Conservation Commissioner Patrick McGowan commented that if the dog were still alive, it had one chance in a million of surviving.

The Allagash Wilderness Waterway is ninety-two miles of lake, shore, and river corridor. Brooks and streams make their way through swamps and wend through thick forests of conifers and northern hardwoods as they work their way to dozens of small lakes and ponds that eventually flow into a river. It is heavily populated by a wide variety of wildlife, including packs of coyotes, which would make short work and a tasty snack out of a lone Labrador wandering through their territory.

On May 29, the day after the accident, Molly was spotted by a game warden at the Gravel Beach campsite on Chamberlain Lake. Later in the afternoon on that same day, she was seen on the Grande Marche Road, twenty miles west of the lake.

Peter Pelletier, the Harmon children's uncle and a state forest ranger, set out for the lake as soon as he learned of the accident and Molly's possible survival. Pelletier was aware that in addition to the coyotes and other predators in the wilderness, the clouds of blackflies are particularly thick at that time of year.

Molly seemed to be everywhere but in safe quarters. Over the next two weeks, the black Lab was sighted by rangers, campers, and fishermen in various places in the Allagash wilderness from Wadleigh Pond, less than twenty miles from the Quebec border, to Scraggly Pond, forty miles in the opposite direction.

Al Cowperthwaite, director of North Maine Woods, received a report that someone working at Caucomgomoc Lake Dam had tried to talk Molly into his truck, but the Lab had bolted. A camper called in a sighting that he had of Molly at Cliff Lake near the Allagash River.

With Molly apparently zigzagging across the wilderness, flyers offering a $200 reward were posted at strategic checkpoints throughout Maine's north woods.

On June 15, Molly arrived at the home of Alain and Bernadette Sirois outside of Millinocket. The Sirois family gave food to the starving dog, but they were completely unaware of the extensive search being conducted for the Lab. They assumed that Molly was a local dog that had wandered away from her family, and they spread the word around Millinocket that they had a lost dog at their home.

Three days later, on June 18, a visitor to Millinocket spotted the "found" poster of the black Lab that the Sirois family had placed in a local florist shop. A call was placed to the North Maine Woods group, which, in turn, contacted Peter Pelletier.

As it happened, Jared Harmon was staying with his grandparents, Mr. and Mrs. Leonard Pelletier, so Peter picked him up on the way to identify the dog that everyone hoped was Molly.

The Sirois family, who were also dog lovers, had cleaned Molly up really well and had removed all the ticks and had treated all her other minor wounds, so Jared was overwhelmed when he saw his father's beloved black Lab looking so well.

Although Molly was still very thin in spite of the Sirois family's generous meals, Jared said it really helped to know that Molly would be returned to the Harmon family.

As Commissioner McGowan told the *Bangor Daily News* (June 19, 2007), "Obviously, we could never bring back their father, but bringing their dog back was something we could do."

Al Cowperthwaite estimated that Molly had traveled well over two hundred miles in twelve days.

And, of course, no one could estimate how many miles that Molly lost in side trips and backtracking. The Allagash Wilderness Waterway and the private and public forestland over which Molly had wandered includes nearly 3.7 million acres in northern Maine.

HOW DID ELLIE MANAGE TO STEER THE HALF-SUNKEN BOAT TO SHORE?

Midafternoon on Friday September 15, 2006, the Auckland Police Maritime Unit picked up a "mayday" distress signal coming from a boat in the Hauraki Gulf off New Zealand. A man we'll call Mr. Fitzgerald signaled that his thirty-foot craft had struck some submerged object three miles off Port Jackson and was rapidly taking on water.

In roughly two hours, two coast guard boats, rescue aircraft, a Westpac Rescue helicopter, and a police copter arrived on the scene, as well as eight private vessels that had picked up Fitzgerald's distress signal. As the rescuers drew near, they could see the man clinging to the submerged hull of his vessel.

Fitzgerald was winched to safety aboard a helicopter. Although he appeared completely uninjured, the rescue craft decided that he should be flown to Auckland City Hospital for a checkup.

As they were headed inland, Fitzgerald asked one of his rescuers if they had seen any sign of Ellie, his border collie.

Since this was the man's first mention that

he had a dog on board with him, the pilot of the copter immediately radioed the boat crews to be on the lookout for a border collie that had also been on board the now-submerged craft.

After a brief and unproductive search, Ellie was presumed dead. A duty officer was told by one of his crew that he thought he had seen a dog in the cabin of the boat just before it had rolled over in a wave. The crewman felt certain that, unfortunately, the dog had drowned inside the cabin.

A more persistent group of rescuers searched the waters for another forty-five minutes without sighting the border collie. Reluctantly, they, too, decided that Ellie had gone down with the ship.

But on Saturday morning, the residents of Great Barrier Island heard some loud and very healthy barking coming from the shore. Those who went to investigate found a very sea-soaked border collie standing astride the wreckage of Mr. Fitzgerald's boat.

A Coast Guard spokesman theorized that when the boat was submerged by the wave one of the rescuers observed sweeping the vessel under the sea, Ellie had managed to find an air pocket in the cabin. Somehow the border collie had traveled ten nautical miles to shore along with pieces of the wreckage.

But the most baffling aspect of Ellie's survival is how she managed to steer or to direct the almost totally submerged vessel to land at Rosalie Bay, just a few minutes from where she lived in Tryphena.

Those curious individuals who went to investigate the vigorous barking at the shore knew Ellie well and brought her home immediately to her favorite couch at the local Irish pub. Once she was settled there, the manager wrapped her in a blanket and drew the couch near the fire so Ellie could dry off.

BRICK FOUGHT TWENTY-FIVE-FOOT WAVES AND SUBZERO COLD ON HECETA ISLAND

They began calling Brick, an eight-year-old Labrador, a miracle dog when it was learned that he had survived twenty-five-foot waves and subzero temperatures for a month.

Brick's owner, Greg Clark, was a forty-eight-year-old beach logger and dog breeder. Folks in southeastern Alaska knew if they saw the big black Lab that Clark wasn't far behind. Brick was always at his owner's side.

On January 22, 2004, Greg and Brick were motoring to the village of Craig to deliver a two-month Labrador puppy to its new owner. Clark's boat, *Katrina*, was a thirty-two-footer, quite sturdily built, but at 12:23 P.M., the experienced seaman sent out a distress call, stating that the seas were soaring to twenty-five feet and that they had struck rocks near Heceta Island.

Fighting the turbulent seas, the rescue crews got to the jutting rocks near Heceta Island as soon as possible. To everyone's dismay, the *Katrina* had been claimed by the angry waters. There was no sign of Greg Clark, Brick, or the puppy.

Rescue crews searched the area for three days before calling it quits. All they had managed to discover was an unused survival suit and various pieces of wreckage.

Greg Clark and his faithful canine companion Brick soon became part of the collective memories and folklore of the southeastern Alaskan seacoast, and they were both remembered with great fondness by all those who knew them.

On February 19, a father and son were fishing off Heceta Island when the older man called his son's attention to the wolf that he had spotted standing on the shore.

Kevin Dau, the younger fisherman, had been a good friend of Greg Clark's, and it took him only a quick look at the shore to recognize the "wolf" as Brick. Since Kevin knew the dog was familiar with him and the sound of his voice, he called Brick's name and urged the Lab to swim for their boat.

Kevin chuckled afterward when he told the story of how Brick had jumped into the sea and swam so fast for the boat that there even seemed to be a wake coming off him.

Brick definitely gave evidence of a month without a good meal. He was very thin and he had injured a leg, but otherwise he appeared in fairly sound condition.

Once Brick was onshore, the townsfolk were in awe of how the Lab had survived for a month without food and shelter in subzero weather.

Someone noted that Brick's fur was matted with tree sap. Perhaps that had picked up some leaves and given him a kind of overcoat. Others suggested that he must have found some bushes under which to crawl to give him some kind of protection. And, of course, there should have been some ground squirrels around for a sparse dinner.

There were those of a mystical frame of mind who thought that the spirit of Greg Clark had stayed around to look after his dog until he was rescued. *Outside Magazine* (September 2004) quoted John Pugh, a friend of Clark's, as saying that he felt Brick's miracle was a kind of message from Greg to the friends he had left behind.

SPICY FOUND
HER OWN SPECIAL ISLAND

Nancy Reynolds of Waterford, Wisconsin, might have expected that Spicy, her little Chihuahua, would have had some of the spice taken out of her by her ordeal, but Reynolds told Kim Dawson (ABC News, August 25, 2002) that Spicy was quickly regaining her full vigor.

On August 13, Reynolds and Spicy were enjoying one of Wisconsin's many waterways in the Milwaukee area on a pontoon boat when the fifteen-pound Chihuahua suddenly fell overboard. All those on board searched desperately for some sign of Spicy, but she was not to be seen anywhere.

Nancy Reynolds remembered that she became hysterical and began to cry. It did not seem possible that one moment Spicy was on board, enjoying the outing, and the next she was nowhere to be seen. Friends were sympathetic, and they extended the search, hoping to catch sight of the Chihuahua paddling toward the pontoon. Spicy was white-haired, so she should have been relatively easy to spot if she had managed to stay afloat after falling off the pontoon.

After many hours, it was obvious even to the grief-stricken Reynolds that the search would have to be abandoned.

Seven days later, maintenance workers found Spicy on Tranquility Island. She had a broken leg and appeared to be exhausted, but the little dog's survival was a miracle in the eyes of Nancy Reynolds.

It was now apparent that Spicy had, of course, survived the fall from the pontoon and had managed to swim three miles to Tranquility Island. There, a veterinarian theorized, the handicapped pooch had managed to survive by eating bugs and an occasional rodent that could not outrun Spicy even with her broken leg.

Nancy Reynolds mused that Spicy seemed to have aged a bit because of her ordeal, but she appeared eager to go on with her life — and perhaps even another pontoon ride.

TRUDI SURVIVED TWO WEEKS AT SEA UNTIL FOUND BY FISHERMEN

In 1990, shortly before the Robert Williamson family of New Zealand left on their vacation, Trudi, their eighteen-month-old rottweiler, had given birth to a litter of puppies. By the time the family departed to cruise along the scenic New Zealand coast in a forty-five-foot boat, the puppies had been either given to their new owners or left in a kennel so that Trudi might also enjoy the trip.

Tragically, it was quite likely while the family was delightedly watching dolphins dancing among the waves that Trudi, still rather exhausted from her recent labors, must have fallen overboard. In all the excitement of attending the boat and observing the dolphins at play, several hours passed before twelve-year-old Aaron noticed that Trudi was missing.

Robert Williamson turned the craft around at his son's first outcry.

They searched and searched for several yards around their boat. Trudi was a big, healthy dog. She should have been able to swim, to keep her head above water.

And then, of course, came the collective guilt. They had been so enchanted by the diving and surfacing dolphins that none of them really knew when Trudi had fallen overboard. In dismal fact, she could have fallen off miles back.

The Williamson family vowed not to abandon the search until they had brought their beloved Trudi back on board. But when darkness came, Robert knew that there was no use looking for their dear rottweiler any longer, and they were forced to head for land.

Later that night, Robert heard Aaron's weeping and listened to his desperate prayers for a miracle to bring Trudi back to him. Robert's own sleep was troubled and restless. He knew that there was no way that Trudi, regardless of her prowess as a swimmer, could last in the ocean.

The next day, over a breakfast that soon grew cold, Robert tried to explain the somber facts of life to his hopeful son. There really was no chance that Trudi had survived the merciless sea. They had no choice but to return home and look after her orphaned puppies that still remained with them. The spirit of Trudi would always live on in her pups.

Two weeks later, however, Aaron received his miracle. A group of fishermen had spotted the rottweiler on an uninhabitable, rocky island. When they found the Williamsons' telephone number on Trudi's dog tags, they called the joyously astonished father and son to come claim their pet.

Veterinary surgeon Murray Gibb agreed that Trudi's survival and rescue definitely fell within the category of the extraordinary. The doctor theorized that extra body fat acquired during pregnancy enabled Trudi to resist the numbing cold of the ocean and helped her to stay afloat during an eight-mile swim to the rocky island.

But once on land, the rottweiler found nothing to eat. Perhaps once again it was the extra body fat accumulated during pregnancy — and generous helpings of food from the Williamsons while on vacation — that enabled Trudi to survive without food for two weeks until she was found by the fishermen.

SNICKERS AND HIS HUMAN FAMILY SHIPWRECKED ON A PACIFIC ATOLL

Snickers, a cocker spaniel, was only five months old when his owners, Jerry and Darla Merrow, set sail from Moss Landing, California, on their forty-eight-foot catamaran in September 2007. Unfortunately, the catamaran developed mast problems not long after setting sail, and the double-hulled vessel drifted on the open sea for ninety-five days until it hit a reef on a small Pacific atoll and ran aground in December.

It was time to abandon ship after three months adrift and the crew — the Merrows, Snickers, and Gulliver, a macaw — swam for Fanning Island, about two hundred yards away.

The Merrows were in luck. A cargo ship had docked at Fanning Island, about a thousand miles south of Hawaii, and they were willing to take the couple on as passengers back to California. However, the captain refused to allow Snickers and Gulliver on board. He told the Merrows that they would have to leave their pets in the care of some of the islanders and arrange later for their transport back to the United States.

Fanning Island is one of thirty-three scattered coral atolls that constitute the remote island nation of Kiribati. Since the Merrows entered the nation without following any kind of official procedure, technically the animals they brought with them were now the property of the government of Kiribati.

It wasn't until they were well out to sea that Jerry and Darla learned from one of the crewmen that the inhabitants of Fanning Island might not have the same concept of keeping animals as pets as did the Merrows. Gulliver, the crewman said, would probably make out all right, but it was not unusual for the folks on Fanning Island to eat dogs.

Although we may be certain that the Merrows felt considerable anguish that their now eight-month-old cocker spaniel might become some islander's dinner, they felt that there was nothing that they could do to prevent such an eventuality if it were to occur. They were shipwreck victims grateful to be on a cargo ship headed back to the States. They could only hope that someone would choose to look after Snickers, rather than to place him in a stew pot.

Robby Coleman, who owned a sailboat and who lived on Fanning Island, soon learned of the plight of Snickers and Gulliver and began to keep an eye on them. In March 2008, he heard that the government of Kiribati had decided that they had provided for the animals long enough and that they had given the Merrows plenty of time to make arrangements to have them transported from Fanning Island. In a few days, they would destroy Snickers and Gulliver.

Coleman managed to contact the Hawaiian Humane Society, who, in turn, sent an e-mail to the Norwegian Cruise Line, asking for a rescue of Snickers and Gulliver. The Hawaiian Humane Society sent pet carriers, flea treatment, and food to the Norwegians, and the cruise line sent a vessel to Fanning Island on April 9 to take the two castaways off the hands of the Kiribati government.

In the meantime, Jack Joslin, a Las Vegas resident, read about the saga of Snickers and Gulliver in a boating journal and called the Hawaiian Humane Society to find out how he could acquire both pets as his own.

Peter Forman, a Hawaii-based airlines historian and a friend of Robby Coleman, heard of the conditions under which the cocker spaniel and the macaw were left on Fanning Island and managed to contact the Merrows. Forman discovered that the Merrows had decided to move on with their lives and were willing to sign a release of ownership so that Joslin might adopt Snickers.

Forman also assisted in negotiating Snickers's transport to Los Angeles. Hawaiian Airlines, touched by the cocker spaniel's great adventure, announced that they would fly Snickers for free to the mainland. There, he would have to undergo a seventy-two-hour quarantine before flying the final lap to Las Vegas.

Snickers arrived at the home of Jack Joslin on Sunday evening, April 20. At first Snickers reacted negatively to the presence of Joslin's twelve-year-old female dog, Missy. Joslin was very understanding regarding the need for a time of adjustment. Snickers had left Moss Landing when he was just a pup. He had drifted on the catamaran with his previous owners for three months, then he was forced to struggle aggressively to stay alive for another four months on Fanning Island. Snickers had weighed about fifteen pounds when he was taken off the island, and after a month with Joslin had packed on another ten pounds of muscle with good food and exercise.

And what of the brave Gulliver? According to Dave Dandoneau of the *Honolulu Advertiser* (April 21, 2008), a plan was under way to move him to Christmas Island and eventually to Los Angeles, one of two American ports to accept exotic birds. Joslin hoped to adopt the macaw, as well.

CAPSIZED AT SEA, BOND AND HIS OWNER TOOK REFUGE ON A DESERTED ISLAND

When Bond, a miniature pinscher, got lost, he had the good sense to do so in the company of his human companion, Melvin Cote — but the circumstances were really quite dangerous. In fact, the two of them got shipwrecked and became castaways in June 2002. And then, according to the *National Post* (June 18, 2002), once they were rescued from a deserted island, the two of them got shipwrecked again and ended up back on the same island.

Cote and Bond had set sail from Prince Rupert, British Columbia, in early June with the intention of spending the summer in the Queen Charlotte Islands. Suddenly, what began as a pleasant excursion became a risky adventure at sea as the weather turned very rough. Cote fought the powerful wind and waves as best he could, struggling to keep their little ship steady and afloat.

Bond, always at his owner's side, fought to stay with Cote, but found his little ten-pound body tossed from one side of the ship to the other.

After a particularly violent smash of the sea against the ship, Cote saw Bond about to fall overboard. He left the wheel to grab Bond and save him from the sea, but his sudden lunge toward the side caused their ship to capsize.

The two companions were thrown into the sea along with all of their supplies and all of their possessions. The waves were too rough to allow them to save anything.

Cote knew their only chance of survival was to swim for the rocks at the northeast tip of Graham Island in Lepas Bay, so with a shout of encouragement to Bond, the two set out, hoping they would be able to reach shore.

Once they found themselves at the rocks, the two shipwrecked sailors found themselves facing another obstacle. Where they had come to shore, the rock face was very steep and required a great deal of effort to climb.

Cote wrenched a shoulder attempting to haul both himself and Bond up to higher ground, and once he got them there, he began to have painful spasms in one of his legs, which made walking farther inland very difficult.

Cote made a quick assessment of their situation: They were both alive, but they had no food and water. They had no radio with which they might signal for help. Since they were independent sorts, no one was expecting them, and only a few friends knew where they were headed.

To their advantage, Cote had been a soldier and had learned survival skills. He knew that they had to stay warm and find some kind of food. He managed to peel bark from some trees and to get a fire going in a sheltered area. There was quite a large growth of fiddlehead ferns on the island and there were mussels clinging to the rock face, so Cote and Bond dined on the scant bill of fare that the island provided. Cote managed to catch rainwater for the two of them to drink.

Helicopters and aircraft frequently passed overhead, but none of them spotted the two marooned survivors, no matter how much Cote waved and shouted and Bond jumped and barked.

On the second day, the castaways were rescued by a group of teachers who were studying sea life at Lepas Bay. Cote and Bond were given a lift to Masset, a small fishing village, located at the northern end of Graham Island.

After taking a couple of days to recuperate, Cote asked a friend of his to take them back to the spot where his ship had sunk in the storm. Nearly everything Cote owned had been aboard that boat, and there might be a chance that if he dove down to investigate, he might be able to salvage some personal possession.

This is the place in the story where things really get weird. Whether by some bizarre accident or some ancient jinx of the sea spirits of Lepas Bay, the second boat began to sink in the exact spot where Cote's vessel had gone under.

Cote later said that something seemed to have got caught in the wheel and there they were, sinking again for the second time in a week.

This time, however, Bond was injured by the incredible circumstances, but Cote pulled him out of the water.

The trio didn't have to bob in the sea for too long a time. A passing ship had seen the boat sink and had alerted the Masset Auxiliary Coast Guard, who arrived shortly and rescued them.

Cote had suffered a separated shoulder on the island, and during the second sinking he had made it worse by pulling Bond out of the water. He told curious reporters that he wanted to be certain that he wasn't jinxed before he set out to sail again. The third time, he reckoned, he and Bond might not be so lucky.

Cote also said that without the companionship of his faithful little Bond, he would easily have become discouraged, marooned on the island without food and water. Although Cote had learned survival skills in the army, it was Bond's indomitable spirit that kept him upbeat and positive that they would survive.

CHAPTER 7
DOGS CARRIED AWAY
BY NATURE'S RAMPAGES

SURVIVING A HURRICANE ISN'T EASY

For years, scientists and environmentalists had been warning everyone they could get to listen that a disaster of biblical proportions was waiting to happen in New Orleans.

In the September 11, 2001, issue of *Popular Mechanics,* an article by Jim Wilson entitled "New Orleans Is Sinking" warned that the surge of a Category 5 storm could put the city eighteen feet under water. Wilson said that if Hurricanes Camille (1969), Andrew (1992), or George (1998) had taken slightly different paths, the French Quarter would have been completely submerged.

In their *National Geographic* article "Gone with the Water" (October 2004), Robert Caputo and Tyrone Turner proved to be eerily prophetic when they described a "broiling August afternoon" when a "whirling maelstrom" would approach New Orleans and more than a million people would have to be evacuated to higher ground. With nearly 80 percent of New Orleans lying below sea level, Caputo and Turner warned, a Category 5 hurricane striking the city would be "the worst natural disaster in the history of the United States."

The wrath of Hurricane Katrina struck New Orleans on August 29, 2005, resulting in "the worst natural disaster" in our nation's history in terms of property damage. Fortunately, the death toll did not reach the numbers predicted by many authorities, and the enormous outpouring of assistance from all areas of the United States, the aid of the Red Cross and civilian and religious relief organizations, plus the efforts of government health agencies all helped ward off a high mortality rate from disease.

Unfortunately, thousands of dogs and other pets died in Hurricane Katrina. Many grieving dog owners were told by their rescuers that they could not take their beloved canine family members with them aboard the boats. Others, who had made it to the New Orleans Superdome on their own to seek shelter, were told that they could not bring their dogs in with them.

As a testament to animal lovers everywhere, authorities reported that 44 percent of pet owners refused to be rescued and chose to stay behind with their pets.

Laura Mahoney, the Louisiana director of the Society for the Prevention of Cruelty to Animals (SPCA), said that she would always remember witnessing the horror of thousands of dogs and cats trying to save themselves by climbing to roofs or high tree branches. Some swam toward boats, but were pushed away to fend for themselves.

Although hundreds of thousands of pets were affected by the storm and admittedly many died, the SPCA estimates that they were able to save about 50 percent of the animals.

Of the 24,000 stray pets left wandering the streets of New Orleans after Katrina subsided, only about 20 percent were returned to their original owners.

But there were miracle stories:

- *Zoey* — Annie Johnson was able to reclaim Zoey, a rottweiler–German shepherd mix, five months after the hurricane. A message seeking word of her pet was posted on the Best Friends' Web site (www.bestfriends.org) and Zoey was located at the St. Francis Animal Sanctuary in Tylertown, Mississippi.

- *Lucky* — It took two years, but Lucky, a bull terrier, was reunited with Roddy Reyes and his family after a Good Samaritan found the dog and brought her into the Miami-Dade County animal shelter.

- *Lassie* — Lois Lerner, who traveled to New Orleans from Maryland purposely to help rescue pets, kept Lassie, an eight-year-old collie, for ten months until her family, the de Rogers, were able to get back on their feet and accept Lassie back into their household.

- *Sheena* — This yellow pit bull terrier was kept from entering the New Orleans Superdome with her owner, John McGee. They were at last reunited in August 2007, two years after the hurricane separated them.

AFTER KATRINA SEPARATED THEM, IT TOOK FOUR YEARS FOR JESSE TO FIND J.J.

It took four years for Jesse Pullins to find J.J. (short for Jesse Junior), the male Labrador-shepherd mix that he had to leave behind when the terrible storm chased Pullins out of New Orleans. Two days before Katrina made landfall, Pullins evacuated his family to Baton Rouge, but before he left he made certain that J.J. had plenty of food and water to hold him over for a few days until he would get back to him. However, when Pullins returned to rescue J.J., he was prevented from entering the city because of an evacuation order.

The story of Pullins and J.J. is unique among the accounts in this book in that after several months of searching and the bereaved owner learning where his missing dog had gone, he had to go to court to have his pet returned to him. After Pullins had appeared on a television program about victims of Katrina waiting to be reunited with their pets, a woman in California who had helped rescue lost and homeless animals in New Orleans realized that she had the paperwork that would match J.J. with an address. J.J. and twenty-eight other dogs that had been separated from their owners by Katrina were sent to the Second Chance at Love Humane Society in Templeton, California. When Pullins contacted the society, he discovered to his dismay that his beloved dog had found a new home in California.

Cheri Lucas, founder of the Second Chance at Love Humane Society, was sympathetic to Pullins's wish to reclaim his dog, but she explained that while she had returned three dogs to their owners on the Gulf Coast, J.J. had been unclaimed for nearly a year after Katrina.

The situation became very difficult because two sisters had adopted J.J. and had come to love him, and they did not want to part with him. Their argument was that they had acquired a dog that they believed had been left without a home after Katrina had swept New Orleans and scattered families and separated them from their pets when their owners moved to other cities to begin new lives.

Pullins initiated a lawsuit to regain ownership of J.J. Intrigued by the court battle that pitted the present owners of a supposedly lost dog with its previous owner, San Francisco–based director and film producer Geralyn Pezanoski made contact with others involved in similar disputes. To her astonishment, she found that there were suits between hundreds of Gulf Coast residents who had lost pets and the animals' present adoptive owners. Ms. Pezanoski interviewed individuals who had lost pets during Katrina and those who had adopted them in good faith. She wanted people to see that the matter was not a simple one to solve. In 2009, Ms. Pezanoski's documentary, *Mine,* won an audience award at the

South by Southwest film festival.

After a year of legal entanglements, the sisters who had adopted J.J. agreed to return him to Pullins in New Orleans. Cheri Lucas said that she was happy about J.J.'s reunion with Pullins, but she was sorry that the two sisters experienced a sad ending to their relationship with the dog. She commented that this was a situation that could have no perfect ending. Somebody had to be hurt by either resolution to the court case.

On June 5, 2009, four years after he had fled with his family to escape Katrina's wrath and reluctantly left his dog behind, Jesse Pullins was reunited with J.J. at the Louis Armstrong New Orleans International Airport.

Bill Haber of the Associated Press quoted Pullins as remarking that J.J. had always been a part of him, a part that had been missing for a long time.

A positive by-product of the tragedy faced by animal owners and their pets during Katrina is that many city and state governments passed legislation regarding pet evacuation. In the future, the efforts involved in saving people will also involve saving their pets.

SURVIVING A TORNADO IS NO PICNIC, EITHER

For those who have not experienced the sudden terror of a tornado, it may seem heartless that in many cases it appears that the family dog was left to fend for itself. But a tornado, unlike a hurricane, does not give advanced warning of its approach. While people may have days to board up their houses or move to safer ground when they learn that a hurricane is blowing toward them, the victims of a tornado may only have at best a few minutes' alarm to find safe shelter. In many instances in a number of the following stories, the families were away from home when the twister struck and were forced to take refuge at the most readily available shelter. In other instances, the dogs may have been confused and frightened by the roar of the violent winds and run off, ignoring the calls to join their families in safe rooms.

THREE WEEKS MISSING, PONGO RETURNED TO FIND TORNADO SPARED HIS DOGHOUSE

Pongo, a nine-year-old basset hound and blue heeler mixed-breed dog, had been missing for nearly three weeks, ever since a tornado damaged Tim and Katresa Harris's home in Gassville, Arkansas, on February 5, 2008. Although Pongo's doghouse had remained standing, his outside pen had been taken away by the terrible winds of the twister. Sadly, the Harris family had to assume that the awful power of the tornado had also taken their dear hound, Pongo.

On Friday, February 22, Katresa Harris left their temporary living quarters and drove to their tornado-wracked home on Kirkland Street to check to see if by some miracle Pongo had returned. Each day since the tornado had struck their home, some member of the Harris family maintained the ritual of checking in on Pongo. Maybe their love and faith would serve as the power that would bring him back to them.

Harris left her car and walked to the backyard where Pongo's house stood silently, awaiting the family's return.

For a moment she felt her dearest expectations may have altered her perceptions, for there, poking his head out of the doghouse, was Pongo. After nearly three weeks of adventures that would never be fully known, the hound had found his way back to his loving family.

Tim Harris told reporter Joanne Bratton of the Mountain View–area paper *Baxter Bulletin,* (February 25, 2008) that Pongo was so excited to see Katresa Harris and to see that his human family had also survived the terrible storm that he left his doghouse on full speed, running to greet Katresa.

NEIGHBORS WITNESSED CHASE TAKEN UP BY TORNADO

During the days after June 7, 2008, Chase, a cairn terrier, and his owner, Sandra Holmes of Richton Park, Illinois, heard a lot of Dorothy and Toto *Wizard of Oz* jokes. On that day, a tornado swept through the neighborhood and picked Chase up from where he was minding his own business in the Holmeses' backyard.

Numerous neighbors witnessed Chase's liftoff. One described the dog's flight as if he were suddenly pulled from the ground and taken up in the air.

Along the street, many friends and neighbors watched in commingled terror and fascination as the terrier appeared to be flying overhead.

Sandra Holmes knows that this story could have had a very unhappy ending, so she declared it a blessing and a miracle from God when the twister set Chase down, dazed and a bit shaken, but very much alive, in the woods a few blocks away.

MASON CRAWLED HOME ON TWO LEGS AFTER DEADLY TORNADO

The spring of 2011 brought a terrible season of deadly tornadoes that wrought awesome destruction on a number of cities. On April 27, a twister flattened much of Tuscaloosa, Alabama, leaving fifty-three dead and thousands homeless and devastated by their losses. President Obama declared a state of emergency for search-and-rescue missions in Alabama.

Mason, a white terrier mix, was home alone when the tornado touched down outside of Birmingham, where he lived with his family. Frightened and confused, Mason cowered in the garage when the winds tore into the home.

When Mason's family returned home from the shelter where they had taken cover during the tornado, they were stunned to find their home now a pile of debris and their little terrier missing. They searched the heavily damaged neighborhood, calling out his name. Depressed over the destruction of their home and grieving over the loss of their dog, the family left.

Three weeks later, they returned to face the sad task of sifting through the piles of debris in search of something of value, perhaps at least some family keepsakes and mementos. They were astonished to find Mason lying there on the shattered porch to greet them. The faithful terrier, his white hair dirty and matted, had crawled home with two broken legs to await their return.

A representative of the Birmingham–Jefferson County Animal Control Shelter told Erin Skarda of TV station MyFox Alabama that the case of Mason crawling home with two broken legs to await his family on the remnants of their destroyed house was probably the most dramatic they had seen in the aftermath of the tornado.

HEROES WORK TO SAVE HUNDREDS OF DOGS DISPLACED IN JOPLIN; DEADLIEST NATURAL DISASTER IN U.S. IN MODERN RECORDS

The death toll of the deadly two-hundred-miles-per-hour tornado that struck Joplin, Missouri, on Sunday night, May 22, 2011, was the highest of any natural disaster in the United States since modern record keeping began in 1950: 160 dead; over 900 injured. Perhaps no accurate statistics will ever be compiled on the number of pets affected by the tornado, but by Wednesday evening, May 25, Karen Aquino, executive director of the Joplin Humane Society, said that they had taken in 370 pets displaced by the monster winds. Some of these animals had been picked up by search-and-rescue teams searching the city's neighborhoods for signs of life. Dogs and cats were brought in with injuries that ranged from scratches and bumps to broken bones to limbs that had to be amputated. But there were many stories of successful rescues, such as the ones recounted by Kelsey Ryan of the *Joplin Globe* (May 25, 2011) and others such as the ones listed below:

- *Betty* — Jay Garrett, a registered nurse from Carbondale, Illinois, traveled to Joplin to volunteer his help in the disaster. As he walked through the terrible destruction in one neighborhood, he found a dog huddled in the ruins of what had once been a family home. That hungry and thirsty dog was later identified as Betty, the dog cherished by the Jeremy Williams family.
- *Bren* — When Jennifer Barber, veterinary staff director of the Joplin Humane Society's Animal Adoption and Resource Center, made a quick appraisal of the pit bull that animal control workers had found on a pile of rubble on Monday, May 23, she estimated that the dog was probably about

twelve hours from death. Bren, the female pit bull, had suffered a gash so deep that it appeared as though someone had taken a butcher knife to her leg. Ms. Barber placed Bren on a heating pad to raise her body temperature, then took her to surgery to attend to her wounds. An hour of stitching was required to reconnect the muscles in the dog's leg.

On Wednesday afternoon, a woman came to the center searching for her two pit bulls that had been carried away by the tornado. She burst into tears when she saw her beloved Bren, covered with scratches, limping from an awful leg wound, but alive and on the mend.

- *Samson* — The Lance family had been out of town when the killer tornado struck, and they returned to find their home completely destroyed. Samson, their chocolate Labrador, was nowhere to be found, and the family feared that he had been killed. Thankfully, rescuers found the Lab trying desperately to stay above water as he paddled in a culvert where he had been blown by the powerful winds.

- *Sugar* — Yet another valiant dog was

this ten-year-old cocker spaniel, found nearly drowned in a drainage ditch. Sugar had trouble treading water because her back legs had been paralyzed. Steven and Debbie Leatherman reclaimed Sugar at a shelter, then their son Daniel drove the dog to the veterinary hospital in Columbia, where spinal surgery was performed that returned the cocker spaniel's use of her legs.

Karen Aquino was grateful to the over a hundred volunteers, including a number of veterinarians, who came to Joplin to help with the animals that had been separated from their owners by the tornado. Ms. Aquino said that none of the homeless animals brought to the Humane Society would be euthanized. She also recognized that many owners had been left with nothing after the destruction had swept the city and that they might not be able to claim their pets. After a certain period of time and allowing for as many inquiries to determine ownership as deemed feasible, some of the animals might be sent to larger cities where their chances of adoption would be greater.

ROXIE CHOSE TO FIGHT THE
TWISTER BY HERSELF

On May 24, 2011, Frank Wood of Piedmont, Oklahoma, took one look at the big twister heading toward his house and realized that he and his two children had only a few minutes to get to their safe room, a heavily fortified shelter in the garage. Seeing his children to safety, Frank called to Roxie, the family dog, to follow them.

Confused by the terrible sound of the powerful wind, Roxie, a tan boxer, refused to enter the safe room.

Wood recalled the awful feeling of having to shut the door behind them, leaving Roxie to meet the violent storm by herself. He tried once more to get the dog to come to him, then, seeing that it was no use to risk his life and that of his children any longer, he gave a silent blessing to Roxie and shut the door behind him.

When he was certain that the tornado had passed over them, Wood and his children left their safe room to look for Roxie. They were shocked when they saw that the top two floors of their three-story house had been blown away. As he surveyed the rubble of their once beautiful house, Wood saw no sign of Roxie. Sadly, it was soon apparent that she may not have fared well, for she was nowhere to be found. Wood cautioned his sorrowful children that they might never see Roxie again.

The next morning, however, their local veterinarian called them with the wonderful news that David Franco, an oil field worker, had found Roxie when he came to work that morning. Roxie had survived having been carried nearly two miles from home by the raging tornado. Happily, the vet told the Woods that the only injury to the resilient Roxie was a scratch on her leg.

PULLED OUT OF THE HOUSE BY THE TORNADO, SHADOW WAS FOUND IN A POCKET OF DEBRIS AFTER FIVE DAYS

When the powerful twister struck Monson, Massachusetts, on June 1, 2011, Shadow, a six-month-old shar-pei-chow mix, was pulled right out of the Carabettas' home. As the startled family rushed to the safety of their basement with their other dog, they were able to hear Shadow's nails dragging across the floor as he tried to resist the tornado's power.

As soon as the wrath of the awful winds left their home, the family began searching for their beloved Shadow, who was especially important to their seven-year-old daughter, Adriana, who had been battling cancer. Audrey Carabetta said that Adriana had struggled with the disease for two years before she entered remission. As soon as she had begun to feel better, Adriana had asked for a puppy. Shadow had been a gift of celebration for the banishing of cancer.

For five heartbreaking days, the Carabettas searched through neighborhood debris and posted signs asking for help in locating Shadow. They had just about given up hope of finding their dog alive when a woman heard barking and whimpering coming from the collapsed roof of the home of Anthony Curtis, a nearby neighbor of the Carabettas. Aware that there was a dog missing, the woman waved down State Trooper Brian Pearl, who went to investigate.

Later, Pearl told the *Boston Globe* (June 5, 2011) that he could see there was a dog buried in the debris under what had been the Curtises' roof. It was obvious to the state trooper that the dog was terrified and did not want to leave the secure pocket in which he had hidden for five days.

After Trooper Pearl unsuccessfully tried luring Shadow out with food, he made the decision to crawl under the pile of debris and pull out the frightened dog with a loop at the end of a pole. Once he got the shar-pei mix free, Pearl told the *Globe,* he began wagging his tail and licking at his rescuer's hand.

Later, Shadow was jumping all over the overjoyed members of the Carabetta family, who matched their dog's enthusiasm in returning to those who loved him.

SADIE WAS AIRBORNE FOR TWO MILES OVER SAGINAW

On September 13, 1993, a tornado touched down in Saginaw, Texas, and carried off shingles, siding, the usual assortment of debris — and one four-pound Yorkshire terrier.

Deputy Sheriff Sandra Davis of the Tarrant County Sheriff's Department received a call at work that the twister had struck her neighborhood, so she telephoned her husband, James, an assistant manager at a local manufacturing plant, and the two of them rushed home.

They were commenting upon how fortunate they were that they had been at work and their eight-year-old daughter, Lindsay, had been at school when they noticed that Sadie, their dog, appeared to be missing.

Their shouts for Sadie soon reached their neighbor Mary Powers, who sadly informed them that she could solve the mystery of the missing terrier. According to her eyewitness testimony, the twister had picked Sadie up and carried her away. Ms. Powers said that she could see the poor little dog "being tumbled around like it was being bounced in a clothes dryer."

Although their house had sustained $60,000 in damage, the Davises' first concern was for their beloved Sadie. Frantically, they searched the countryside near their neighborhood, praying that, somehow, the tornado might have set the little terrier down safely somewhere in the area.

Freely expressing their sentiment that Sadie was a member of their family, the Davises sorrowfully had to call off their unsuccessful search by evening. No one wanted to put into words what appeared to be the realistic conclusion: They would never again see their dear little Sadie.

But a miracle occurred the very next day. A man who lived more than two miles away called the Davis family to inform them that the dog that he had found after the storm was wearing tags that identified her as their pet.

Within minutes, Deputy Davis and her husband had driven the two miles that separated them from Sadie and they reclaimed their windblown, but unharmed, Yorkshire terrier.

Believed to be Killed by an Explosion During the L.A. Earthquake, Bimbo Miraculously Returns Three Days Later

Bimbo, a five-year-old German shepherd, was blinded and burned beyond recognition in an explosion that followed the devastating Los Angeles earthquake in January 1994. Although her owner, Jim Menzi, had assumed that she had been consumed by the flames, she miraculously survived the deadly inferno.

Menzi's truck had stalled at an intersection flooded by a broken water main during those frightening moments after the quake. His two canine buddies, Shep and Bimbo, were with him in the cab when he tried to start his vehicle.

What Menzi could not know was that there was a natural gas leak nearby that had been caused by the tremors of the deadly quake, and when he turned the key in the ignition, the gas connected with the spark and exploded.

Instinctively, Menzi jumped from his burning truck and into the water that surrounded it. He assumed that his dogs would follow his lead and abandon ship, but when he heard their terrible wails and yelps of pain and fear, he realized that the flames were holding them back.

Sadly, helpless to do anything to aid them in their escape, all Menzi could do was to pray that Shep and Bimbo would die as quickly and as painlessly as possible.

Later that day, when he was taken to a hospital, it was discovered that Jim had burns on 30 percent of his body. Rushed to intensive care, he mourned his dogs' fate.

Menzi told journalist William Keck that he kept replaying in his mind the nightmarish explosion that had claimed his dogs. He could still hear their pathetic howls.

But three days later, Menzi received the astonishing news that Bimbo had somehow managed to survive the fire in the pickup. She had been found temporarily blind and completely helpless, wandering in someone's yard, when a fireman noticed her and took her to a veterinarian. All evidence indicated that Shep had died in the fire.

From his hospital bed, Menzi called the vet and inquired about his beloved Bimbo's well-being. The German shepherd had sustained burns covering nearly 70 percent of her body. She would have to continue to fight to live.

Menzi gave thought to the humane consideration that it might be better to put her to sleep. The confident veterinarian reminded him that the doctors at the hospital had not put *him* to sleep.

Inspired by the vet's bravado, Menzi resolved that he would not allow Bimbo to die. He arranged to talk to his dog via speaker-phone, and he told Bimbo that he loved her. The nurse who was with the German shepherd at the Blue Cross Pet Hospital said that every time Menzi spoke, Bimbo licked her hand.

Both master and dog underwent similar treatments for their burns.

As soon as he was released after sixteen days in the hospital, Menzi headed for the pet hospital to be with Bimbo.

The attending veterinarians had shaved what patches of hair had not been burned in the pickup fire, and her paws were swollen and bleeding, but to Menzi's eyes, Bimbo had never looked more beautiful.

Later he told writer Keck that he had never felt a stronger bond with his dog. "Bimbo and I have been given the gift of life, and we're going to live each day for all it's worth."

CHAPTER 8
DRAMATIC RESCUES

SKITTISH SHELTIE EVADED RESCUE FOR FOUR MONTHS

Christina and Jamie Guitard and daughter Katy Thibodeau were cautioned by the dog breeder before they accepted the care of Walker, a sheltie, that the dog was a bit skittish. Shelties, also known as Shetland sheepdogs, are very intelligent dogs, well known for their gentle and sweet disposition, but the breeder decided to sell Walker when he proved to be too shy around other trainers and their dogs. She had hoped to train Walker to be a show dog, but he had such a reticent personality that he was unable to compete in any major events. Walker had done extremely well in the obedience classes leading up to the show ring, but he was just too timid and non-competitive to be effective against the other dogs.

In addition to issuing the warning about Walker's shy nature, the breeder also advised the Guitards and Ms. Thibodeau that Walker had been placed in two previous homes, but each time had been returned to her for various reasons. The breeder said that Walker was now four years old, and because the breed is widely known as an excellent companion animal, she promised that he should respond to the love and special attention that she was certain he would receive from their family.

The sheltie has a long and thick double coat with a full frill around the neck area, so the Guitards soon discovered that Walker would need extensive grooming and require it on a regular basis. The breed, originally bred to be herders of livestock, also requires a lot of brisk exercise.

In October 2007, a deliveryman came to the Guitards' home in Hants, Nova Scotia, and Christina noticed at once that Walker began acting nervous.

Perhaps there were too many voices speaking at once. Or maybe the deliveryman reminded Walker of one of his previous owners who may have abused him. Whatever the cause, Walker saw that the front door was open, and he bolted.

Before any family member completely realized what was happening, Walker was gone. And he remained gone for four months, right through the cold winter months.

Immediately when he fled the Guitards' home, Walker was spotted along the railway tracks, but no one was fast enough to grab him by his collar, and no one was commanding enough to order him to go home.

The Guitards distributed missing-dog posters throughout the area, including Windsor, Fairmouth, and Hantsport. Individuals called in with dozens of sightings, but no one could catch the elusive sheltie.

Some concerned individuals who thought they had spotted Walker mapped areas where he was seen the most often, and the Guitards set a humane trap near one of them. Sadly, in this instance, the dog's great intelligence worked against their being able to catch him.

When Christina Guitard arranged for a consultation with the animal control center, she was advised that there was little hope of catching the shy Walker. Although she refused to abandon her dog, she had to concede that the winter months were fast approaching and that there would be little chance of Walker surviving the hungry coyotes — and his own hunger.

She knew that the sensible thing to do would be to forget the skittish sheltie and simply obtain another dog. Friends tried to convince her that it had been several weeks since anyone had spotted Walker. Common sense dictated that he was dead.

But then, in the dead of winter, people began spotting Walker once again. The Guitards received calls from people who said that they were leaving food out for the runaway dog.

For a time, reports came in with numerous sightings near the Bog Road, so the Guitards drove out there with the intention of setting a trap for Walker that would be too tempting to resist. Jamie built a small campfire in the wilds and began to fry bacon, hoping the familiar scent of a favorite food would bring Walker on the run for home and regular meals.

The aroma wafting through the woods seem to be working its intended magic when Christina caught sight of Walker at the edge of the forest. She called out to him that it was time that he came home with them.

But the sheltie seemed confused by their actions and cries, and he turned back into the woods and disappeared.

Finally, not long after the tempting scent of bacon had failed to bring Walker home, the Alison family, who lived in the neighborhood and had noticed a strange dog circling their property, set a humane trap and baited it with a roast beef dinner.

That night Mrs. Alison called the Guitards with the news that they had been waiting four months to hear. Walker was in the Alison home and waiting to be taken home by his owners.

When Christina arrived to take him home, she picked Walker up and held him in her arms. She told people later that he was as light as feather, just skin and bones.

An examination by a veterinarian produced a diagnosis that with the exception of being malnourished, an infected paw, and a heart murmur, Walker was in good shape.

Perhaps the terrible ordeal of wandering in the winter cold had served as a kind of period of emotional growth for Walker. Christina could not help observing how calm he now seemed to be. She said that she could almost see a kind of relief in his eyes, as if he had at last outrun and outlasted the emotional fears that so troubled him before he ran out to face the unknown.

Nadine Armstrong reported in the *Hants Journal* that the Hants County SPCA had become so touched by the Guitards' tenacity in retrieving their sheltie that they had decided to cover the expenses of Walker's medications.

TALES OF TWO
BERNESE MOUNTAIN DOGS
Hurley was Missing for Fifteen Days

Hurley, a Bernese mountain dog, was rescued after being lost for fifteen days in British Columbia's North Shore Mountains. Darwin Schandor, Hurley's owner, expressed his gratitude to the hundreds of people who had searched for the eighteen-month-old dog and to the aerial team from North Shore Rescue that had brought him to safety from a ledge in a heavily wooded area in North Vancouver.

The Schandor family had been on a spring break vacation in Maui, Hawaii, on March 24, 2011, when they received an upsetting telephone call from the pet service that they had hired to look after their dog. Paul Riley, the owner of Embark Dog Centre, informed them that Hurley had run off and gotten lost on the Baden Powell Trail.

But what about the GPS tracking collars that the service placed on the dogs when they walked them? The Schandors had used the service in the past because they knew that their walkers always attached a GPS collar on Hurley.

Riley told Darwin and his wife, Tracie, that because Hurley was always so well-behaved on the mountain hikes, no collar was used on this particular outing. He also added that the employee who was accompanying Hurley when he disappeared was one of their most experienced.

The Schandors and their two children — ten-year-old son Hudson and eight-year-old daughter Kiana — returned to Vancouver to begin a search for their beloved dog that would stretch into two weeks. Paul Riley and hundreds of volunteers joined Darwin Schandor in daily searches for the missing dog. Schandor and others devoted to finding Hurley often put in twelve- to fifteen-hour days. The North Shore Rescue personnel provided the searchers with maps and advice on how best to cover the heavily wooded area where the dog was likely to be found. A Facebook group was launched for people in the area to report any possible sightings, and within a few days it had over six hundred members.

On Thursday, April 7, a hiker spotted Hurley near Mosquito Creek. Although it was by fortunate chance that the man sighted Hurley, Tim Jones, the North Shore Rescue search manager, had a hunch all along that the dog was somewhere in that area.

The rescue team found the dog on a ten-foot-wide ledge beside a water source at an elevation of 1,800 feet. It seemed likely that Hurley had fallen and tumbled down to the ledge. The rescuers assessed that the dog was not badly injured, except for a scratched paw. They also judged that it was too risky to send rescuers in on foot to try to retrieve Hurley from the ledge.

Flight team members Mike Danks and Jeff Yarnold flew in by helicopter and were lowered down to Hurley by a two-hundred-foot-long cable to accomplish a dramatic and safe rescue of the dog. Once they had coaxed Hurley into the harness at the launch area at the Cleveland Dam, just south of Capilano Lake, he was lifted into the air to dangle between the two men on the flight to Vancouver.

Darwin Schandor was waiting to welcome his dog home. Hurley appeared to be in good shape in spite of his ordeal. It was obvious that he had lost weight; his weight was later confirmed by a veterinarian to be 90 pounds, 25 pounds below his normal weight of 115.

Schandor told Kim Pemberton of the *Vancouver Sun* (April 8, 2011) that it had been a tough two weeks. Every night their children would go to bed crying over Hurley's disappearance. After so many days missing, the family had begun to think that they would never again see their dog. Now that Hurley had returned, Schandor vowed, the family would never go on another vacation without taking him along.

Sasha Went Over a Cliff While Chasing a Mountain Goat

Another Bernese mountain dog had to be rescued in July 2011 when Gwen Hall and Jim Krieger were climbing with Sasha, heading toward the 5,944-foot summit of Mount Elinor in Washington's Olympic Mountains. The climb was going well until Sasha spotted a mountain goat and began to give chase.

Gwen Hall told the *Bellingham Herald* that their Bernese mountain dog bolted after the goat and in the matter of a few seconds disappeared over a cliff. Hall called and whistled for their dog, but assessing the situation and estimating that Sasha had fallen nearly 150 feet, she began to fear the worst.

When they had not found Sasha after three days, Hall and Krieger contacted Olympic Mountain Rescue, a volunteer mountain rescue team, which sent six search specialists to assist them in locating the five-year-old dog. After five hours, the *Herald* reported on July 26, the team found Sasha lying motionless on her side on a very narrow mountain shelf. Expertly, the rescue specialists hauled Sasha up to safety.

Remarkably, the desperate and dangerous goat pursuit, the 150-foot fall, and the three days lost from her anxious owners had only cost Sasha a broken tooth and an injured paw.

MISSING FOR NINE DAYS, GALE WAS FOUND IN A VERY STRANGE PLACE

Under her pen name of Elizabeth Buchannan, Tamar Jones has made her dog, Gale, a popular literary character in England by writing about her canine adventures on the farm. Since Jones and her ten-year-old border collie live near the village of Fylingthorpe near Whitby, North Yorks, the magazine articles extol the virtues of country living. Jones has also authored a full-length book entitled *Seasons at Sunnyside* about rural life in the company of a beloved canine companion. The tranquil existence the two of them shared on the farm appeared to be idyllic and free of any stress or woe.

Until the day in late October 2007 that Gale disappeared.

After an intense search of the surrounding farms and countryside, Tamar Jones came to the unthinkable conclusion that Gale had either been killed or kidnapped, for she was certain that there was no way that her beloved pet would run away. Many of the villagers encouraged her not to give up hope, and they joined in the search for Gale, who was, after all, a famous personality in the area.

As the days stretched agonizingly from one to many, Jones was about to give up all hope of once again seeing her beloved Gale.

Then, on the ninth day after Gale disappeared, Jones was startled by a local farmer tapping on her window and shouting that he had Gale with him in the trunk of his car.

Jones knew that the man had been on holiday in London, so she was completely puzzled as to why he would have her missing dog in his trunk.

She followed him out to his car and looked in the trunk of his Vauxhall Astra, and there, looking very weak, stiff, and unwell, was Gale. With the farmer's help, Jones gently lifted Gale out of the trunk and set her on the ground.

As she was pouring a basin of water for the dog, who appeared to have an unquenchable thirst, Ms. Jones reflected back on the farmer's final visit to her place before he left for London.

The man often did odd jobs for her, and she was helping him unload some supplies from his trunk when an airplane flew low overhead. Gale had always had a fear of airplanes, and she'd jumped into the farmer's trunk and put her paws over her ears.

According to Tamar, Gale has never liked any unwelcome noises, such as that caused by an airplane buzzing low over the farm, so she assumed that after the dog had covered her ears for a bit, she had run off to hide somewhere that she considered to be safe. Tamar clearly remembers looking into the trunk of the Vauxhall Astra and seeing that the last bit of supplies had been removed. What she did not know was that Gale had curled up and huddled behind a toolbox where she could not be seen.

For seven days, Gale had lain in the farmer's trunk while he was off on a week-long holiday in London to spend time with friends. When he returned home, all the talk in the village about Tamar Jones's missing dog had pretty much died down. If he had heard the sad news, he would undoubtedly have called on Jones to express his sympathy.

Two days later, when he finally decided to clean out his car, he opened the trunk and was astonished to see a very anguished Gale lying behind the toolbox.

At first, he called to her to free herself from the "boot," as the trunk is called in England, but Gale was too weak to move. Without wasting another moment, he drove directly to Tamar Jones's farm to declare that her dear Gale was in his trunk and that she had been there since her scare by the low-flying airplane nine days ago.

After their amazing reunion and after Gale had been allowed to drink until satisfied, Ms. Jones took her immediately to the veterinarian.

The doctor was perhaps even more astonished than Tamar had been. The longest that a dog had been known to survive without food was two weeks, but a canine cannot exist without water for more than two days. There had to have been some condensation in the trunk of the car for Gale to lick or it would have been completely impossible for her to have survived.

The veterinarian theorized that once Gale had understood the situation in which she found herself, she had shut her body down to conserve energy. Dogs cannot enter an actual stage of hibernation, like that of a bear, but they can enter into a very similar type of period of diminished functions if they need to do so, and that is what Gale must have done. She shut down nearly all her bodily processes in order to keep her blood pumping.

All of Tamar Jones's rural neighbors and the helpful folks in the village were delighted when, after a period of recuperation, Gale was once again her old lively self, jogging happily along at the side of her owner.

TRAPPED IN A STORM DRAIN FIFTEEN FEET UNDERGROUND

In August 2007, Alex, a dalmatian, was trapped fifteen feet underground in an old storm drain for four days, but his loving owners, the Thomson family of Wayne County, West Virginia, certainly did not bury him on purpose nor by accident. For fourteen years, Alex had been an integral part of their family, and the Thomsons dug for days in an attempt to free their beloved dog.

At first the family was baffled when old Alex disappeared. They searched desperately for four days before they heard him whimpering from far below their feet. The old guy had crawled down a tunnel to an old storm drain in an effort to cool off in the West Virginia heat. And then, it was painfully obvious, he had become stuck — fifteen feet below.

The whole family began to cry tears of joy at having found their faithful old dalmatian after conducting a wide search of the area surrounding their home, but the tears of relief were quickly transformed to ones of dread when they fully realized that Alex was stuck in a tunnel deep underground and that they had no way of extricating him from the earthen trap.

The elder Thomson decided to waste not another minute. Old Alex had been lying down there in the darkness for four days without a bite to eat. He picked up a shovel and started digging.

He was still at it two days later when a neighbor with a backhoe heard of the Thomsons' dilemma and their attempts to rescue Alex. The friend was an expert at working the machine with its massive iron claw, and he knew that if he got too close to the dog, the claw could easily rip Alex in half.

At last, after two days of digging, the backhoe had made a hole large enough and deep enough to enable the Thomsons to wedge themselves and a ladder down to the storm drain and allow them to free Alex.

Pet Project (August 21, 2007) stated that as soon as the crew got the dalmatian to the surface, they placed him on a stretcher and got him to the veterinarian, where he was pronounced in miraculously good condition after his ordeal in the underground storm drain.

A Blind Pekingese Endures Two Months in a Well

According to a report in *China Daily* (November 23, 2011), Doudou, a two-year-old blind Pekingese, survived two months trapped in an uncovered well. Doudou's owner, Meng Shasha, a twenty-six-year-old finance worker from Qingdao, a coastal city in Shandong Province, was on a business trip when the dog went missing. Meng had adopted him from a friend in 2009, and she had left him in the care of another friend when she left home in October. When she returned in early November, she was dismayed when her friend told her that Doudou had gotten out and wandered away.

Meng searched the streets, put up posters, and posted messages on the Internet. Whenever she looked at Doudou's pictures, she would burst into tears.

While Meng spent every available moment away from her work searching the streets and alleys of Qingdao, Wang Bin, a reporter on the staff of *Peninsula City News,* received a call from a reader concerning the plight of a dog that had been trapped at the bottom of a well for over twenty days. According to the caller, people had been tossing food scraps to the little Pekingese to keep it alive. Although no one had tried to rescue the dog, the people living and working in the neighborhood were trying to do what they could.

Deciding to investigate what might be a good human-interest story, Wang contacted a veterinarian who agreed to accompany him to the site.

The two men tried their best to hook the Pekingese with a box tied to a rope, but they were unsuccessful in their efforts to pull the little dog out of the well.

Wang published the story in the paper the next day and received more than two hundred comments from readers.

Meng saw the report on November 9 and knew that the little Pekingese was her Doudou. Wang gave her the location of the well, which Meng was astonished to learn was outside of a gas station not far from her home. There were over ten uncovered wells in proximity to one another. Each was only a little over six feet deep, so it appeared that while passersby were sympathetic enough to the dog's plight to toss it some food, no one wished to take the time to enter the well and free the Pekingese from its prison.

As soon as the blind dog heard his owner's voice, he became excited, barking loudly and jumping as high as he could toward the familiar sound of Meng's voice.

Meng did not hesitate to lower herself into the well. At first the sounds of the curious crowd who had assembled to witness the rescue caused Doudou to shrink back. But when Meng reached out her hand for Doudou to sniff, the dog whined, licked her fingers, and came into her loving arms.

After a visit to the veterinarian for a health check and a bath, Doudou was very happy to be home after two months in that dismal well.

Meng Shasha told reporters Wang Bin and Xie Chuanjiao that before he went missing, she had never allowed Doudou in her bedroom. Now she had given him a mattress to sleep on right next to her bed.

RABBIT HOLES CAN BE HAZARDOUS TO A DOG'S HEALTH: BILBO WAS TRAPPED IN A MAZE FOR TWENTY DAYS

Most often when you hear about a dog disappearing underground, you can almost always assume that he or she was chasing a smaller animal into its burrow.

On November 7, 2011, seven-year-old Bilbo, a border cross–lakeland terrier mix, confidently chased a rabbit into a hole — and then found himself unable to get back out. Bilbo had been walking across Bodmin Moor, near the home that he shared with his owners, the Harwood family, when he spotted the rabbit that seemed to be asking to be chased. Bilbo charged into the hole, sensing an immediate capture of his prey, only to find himself lost and stuck in an underground maze.

Nicky Harwood sought help from the local firemen, but they told her that the tunnel might collapse if they started to dig into it. She would just have to wait until Bilbo managed to find his own way out.

Harwood, her husband, Andy, and their two children, Perry and Georgina, brought bowls of food down to the rabbit hole and tried to coax Bilbo out with the aromas of his favorite dishes. After several hours of calling to their pet, they gave up for the evening, but they promised Bilbo that they would return the next day.

The Harwood family visited the rabbit hole for a few hours every day for over two weeks, bringing with them a variety of familiar-smelling items that they hoped would inspire Bilbo to dig his way out of his prison. They sat hopefully outside the bunny's home with Bilbo's bed, his favorite foods, even the family's bedsheets in concerted efforts to inspire him to dig his way to freedom.

After twenty days, Bilbo had lost enough weight to squeeze his way out of the rabbit warren and wiggle his way to freedom. He walked to the lot where his family had parked their car nearly three weeks before and began to look around, reexamining the world outside of Middle Earth. It was not long before a passer-by recognized him from the missing dog posters that the Harwoods had posted and called the family.

Nicky Harwood recalled for the *Daily Mail* (November 2, 2011) that Bilbo was caked in mud and had difficulty breathing. He looked skinny, but a veterinarian's examination determined that Bilbo weighed only three and a half pounds less than he did when he decided to enter the world of rabbits. The veterinarian theorized that Bilbo had survived from eating soil and deriving both a little water and nourishment from that unpleasant diet.

The Harwoods were thankful that their dog had survived his adventure in tunnel exploration, and they felt they had been blessed with a miracle when Bilbo returned to them.

JAKE WAS AN UNWILLING GUEST OF RABBITS FOR TWENTY-FIVE DAYS

There must be a number of hazardous zones in the UK that are scattered with numerous rabbit holes to tempt small dogs to enter their dangerous mazes. In May 2009, six-year-old Jake, a Jack Russell terrier owned by Jill and Richard Thomas of West Wales, was trapped in a rabbit warren for twenty-five days before he managed to escape by losing enough weight to crawl out. Although his owners admitted that Jake had been overweight on the day he disappeared while walking with Richard, the terrier was decidedly the worse for wear when he freed himself from a near-starvation diet. Jake had lost about a quarter of his body weight and had to be placed on a drip to ensure his survival.

JUDY WENT DOWN THE RABBIT HOLE FOR THIRTY-SIX DAYS

The endurance champ for surviving entrapment in a rabbit warren is another Welsh dog, the indomitable Judy, a ten-month-old terrier, who survived an astounding thirty-six days trapped underground in a rabbit hole.

It had begun as an ordinary afternoon walk around the family farm for eleven-year-old Evan Davies on that summer's day in 1990. Judy was dashing ahead in the field near the Davies home in Powys, Wales. Spotting a rabbit, the feisty terrier pursued the bunny to its "front door" — as she so often did — but this time she went right on inside Mr. Rabbit's home.

Evan was left standing there openmouthed with shock. Judy had often chased the rabbits to their holes, then bounded away to find new game when the long-eared creatures disappeared into their warrens. Judy had never before taken her pursuit to the rabbits' private domain.

Evan called and called for his pet to return, then ran off sobbing to enlist the help of his mother and sister. That night, after work, Evan's father joined the search for the missing dog.

Although the eleven-year-old boy maintained his faithful vigil for his beloved terrier for several days, his parents tried to console him with promises of obtaining another Judy. Blinking back his tears, Evan stoutly insisted that there could never be another Judy — and he knew that somehow she was still alive.

A month later, Malcolm Davies asked his son if he would reconsider the offer of a new puppy. He told Evan that he must face the sad truth of the matter that Judy might never come back to him.

Evan knew his father meant well, but he asked everyone to wait a little longer. "Judy might show up," he said, more as a plea.

Incredibly, it was only a week later that John Gordon, one of the Davieses' neighbors, was awakened at midnight by the sound of a dog barking. Somehow Gordon knew that it was Evan's missing terrier.

About half a mile from his home, Gordon found a skinny, half-starved dog attempting to claw its way out of a rabbit hole. He dug the terrier free with his bare hands, then gave her some food and water. He permitted her only a few moments to rest, then he put her in his car and drove her home to the Davieses' farm.

Malcolm and his wife awakened their son with the joyful news that Judy had returned from her thirty-six-day sojourn in the kingdom of the rabbits. Evan jumped from his bed, laughing and sobbing in uncontrollable delight.

Later, an examining veterinarian found that except for a minor eye infection, Judy was surprisingly none the worse for wear after her five-week ordeal. He theorized that the stubborn terrier managed to survive on her own body fat, perhaps a slaughtered rabbit, plant roots, and insects. She must also have found some underground water.

Evans set about fattening up his remarkable pet so that Judy would become so plump she wouldn't be able to squeeze down any more rabbit holes.

BACK TO LIFE
AFTER PREMATURE BURIALS

We end this chapter with accounts of two dogs who experienced another kind of underground entrapment when they found themselves the victims of premature burials.

Brandy

In October 1992, Patricia Corcoran of Botwood, Newfoundland, had to face up to the sad fact that her ten-month-old mongrel dog, Brandy, was dead. Patricia acquired Brandy when she was just a six-week-old puppy, and Brandy had always been a very good pet, loyally following Patricia and her daughters everywhere. But now, since Patricia could no longer feel a heartbeat in her loyal little companion, she would have to accept Brandy's death as a sad reality of life.

Patricia asked a friend to assist her in Brandy's burial, and they chose a lovely spot near a waterfall. They dug a three-foot grave, said a few words, thought a few kind thoughts, and returned to Botwood.

Eleven days later, Patricia happened to catch a public-service message on the local television station that described a lost dog that perfectly fit Brandy's description.

When she called the number and asked the man who had found the lost dog to call her "Brandy," he said that the dog had become very excited and began to jump up and down.

Patricia drove to the spot where they had buried Brandy, and she was stunned to find a hole in the grave, where the dog had apparently dug herself free.

When she went to reclaim her pet, Patricia was further stunned to learn that Brandy had been found only four days after she had mistakenly buried her.

The veterinarian who later examined Brandy theorized that she had only become unconscious prior to her premature burial. After a few days of good food and tender loving care, Brandy appeared to be doing fine and bore no sign of any grudge that she had awakened in a three-foot hole in which her owner had covered her with dirt.

Eddie

Blind and deaf Eddie, a fifteen-year-old bearded collie–poodle mix, had recently experienced a stroke. His devoted owner, Dianne Slater, had raised Eddie since he was three days old and had bottle-fed him as a puppy.

When Eddie disappeared on August 16, 2005, Dianne was baffled. Where could a deaf and blind dog who had recently survived a stroke go? Dianne and her family searched all the streets near their home in Pildacre Lane, Ossett, UK, but their efforts were in vain. Eddie was simply nowhere to be found.

Slater couldn't sleep at all that night. She lay thinking of her beloved pet. She was convinced that she would never see him again. It seemed logical to assume that the valiant Eddie, deaf, blind, hindered by a recent stroke, had simply collapsed somewhere and that she would never see him again.

Strangely enough, the following day the Slaters learned that Eddie had experienced a premature burial of sorts. He had fallen into a five-foot-deep dike a few miles away in Earlsheaton, near Dewsbury, and had been trapped. To add to the difficulty of tough, old Eddie climbing out of the dike, workmen, not spotting the dog, had dumped a pile of rubble on top of him.

It wasn't until the next morning in full daylight that a crew of workers heard a dog's muffled barking and spotted him covered with rubble. They dug Eddie out of his impromptu grave and brought him to the police station.

A delighted Dianne Slater thanked the police and the workmen and vowed to keep a closer watch on her dear old Eddie. She admitted that he had been a bit of an escape artist, a kind of canine Houdini, when he was much younger, but she had thought those days were far behind him.

CHAPTER 9
DOGS THAT FOUND
THEIR OWNERS AGAINST
IMPOSSIBLE ODDS

PETER DIDN'T HAVE A
TICKET TO RIDE, BUT HE STILL
FOUND HIS OWNER

In his extraordinary book *Man's Best Friend: The Story of the Dog* (1928), Captain Albert H. Trapman tells of the remarkable adventures of Peter, a bull terrier, who somehow managed to change trains and comprehend complicated time schedules in order to travel back and forth between Cairo and Upper Egypt in search of his master.

About 1901, a Mr. Jobson, a British government official, was stationed in Upper Egypt.

An efficient and congenial fellow, Jobson was also known for his propensity to bring his dog with him wherever he traveled. Jobson's friends were often amused by the bull terrier's serious demeanor and the manner in which he would settle himself comfortably in a train seat and never once even glance out a window — even during the fifteen-hour journey to Cairo.

A career reassignment transferred Jobson to Damanhur, a city about three hours from Cairo, and on one occasion, he received word that a situation had arisen in which it was absolutely necessary for him to leave for Cairo immediately. Jobson was unsettled by the demands of the order, but he had no choice but to comply at once — and that meant that he would have to leave without Peter.

Although his faithful bull terrier had become as much a facet of his overall appearance as his necktie, briefcase, and walking stick, Jobson bade Peter a hasty farewell minutes before he left for the train station, hoping that his usual traveling companion would understand why he had to be left behind on this trip.

The colleagues Jobson had asked to look in on his dog were quick to observe that he had left behind a very grumpy and out-of-sorts bull terrier — but they didn't know the half of what was churning over in Peter's canine mind. It seemed that the resentful Peter reasoned that Jobson must have returned to their former home in Upper Egypt, and he could not imagine why his master would leave him behind. Well, decreed the unhappy bull terrier, he would remedy that awful oversight. He would set out straightaway and surprise Jobson by joining him there.

Somehow Peter made his way through the streets of Damanhur and managed to get on board a train to Cairo. Once he reached that familiar destination, he was able to change platforms, switch trains, and set out on the fifteen-hour ride to their old post in Upper Egypt.

Although Jobson's human traveling companions had often observed that Peter had never bothered to look out the window during his many previous trips back and forth to Cairo from Upper Egypt, some uncanny power of mind told the determined bull terrier when to leave the train and where to go to search out Jobson's old haunts at his previously assigned station.

Perplexed when he could not locate his master at his old station on business, Peter's bull terrier logic convinced him that Jobson must rather be visiting some friends in Cairo. Without wasting any more time, he headed once again for the train depot and the long ride back to Cairo.

Fifteen or so hours later, Peter was seen poking his head in the doors of a number of Jobson's friends and acquaintances in Cairo.

Time and time again, startled men and women asked the bull terrier what on earth he was doing there in Cairo. And where in the world was Jobson? What was Peter doing without his master at his side?

When he was unable to discover Jobson at any of the familiar ports of call, Peter displayed visible disappointment. He accepted water and food from a few thoughtful friends, but he summarily resisted their efforts to keep him in one place. Where on earth, indeed, was that naughty, inconsiderate, wandering Jobson?

Incredibly, the resourceful bull terrier once again made his way back to the Cairo train depot, waited patiently for three hours for the correct train to arrive, then entrained once more for Damanhur. (The authors of this book braved the Cairo train depot in the 1980s, and the mass confusion there is quite enough to tax the most patient and persevering of human travelers, to say nothing of a bull terrier.)

Once back in Damanhur, the persistent Peter was at last rewarded for his tireless, nearly forty-eight-hour search for his master. Jobson had returned home and had been worried sick about the mysterious disappearance of his loyal dog.

Although this incredible story may sound

like an inspired piece of clever fiction, the details were confirmed by a careful inquiry conducted by Jobson and his friends, many of whom had observed Peter at various locations during his determined quest to locate his master throughout Upper Egypt and Cairo.

PRINCE FOUND HIS OWNER IN THE TRENCHES OF WORLD WAR I

The tale of the indomitable Prince, a collie-Irish terrier mix, has survived many a telling and retelling from the days of World War I, but it still remains a classic that has inspired generations of dog lovers.

Jimmy Brown joined the British Army during the onset of hostilities and left his family, including Prince, with relatives in Hammersmith, London. Brown's unit was among the earliest British contingents to be sent over the English Channel, and he was soon in France, immersed in the thickest of the fighting in the trenches.

After a brutal time amidst the barbed wire, the mud, and the blood, Brown was permitted a brief leave to visit his family in London. When, all too soon it seemed, it was time for him to return to the front, his feisty collie–Irish terrier would have none of it. At first Prince moped, refused all food, and barely drank enough water to stay alive. Then he decided to take matters into his own paws.

Colleen Brown was shocked when she stepped outside one morning to look after Prince and made the terrible discovery that he was gone. She looked everywhere.

She was distraught, sick with worry. Prince had always been such an obedient dog, and now she must break the awful news in a letter to Jimmy that his beloved friend had run away.

After thinking the situation over, Colleen decided to wait ten days before she made the formal declaration to her husband that Prince had disappeared. She didn't want to do anything to demoralize Jimmy, knowing that he was suffering enough in the cold, wet trenches in France, crouching for safety from deadly German machine-gun fire. In those ten days, she vowed, she would exert every effort to attempt to track down the missing dog.

Sadly, the ten days passed without a sign of Prince. Nothing had been gained by the delay, and Colleen came to the dismal understanding that all she had accomplished in the interim was to make a pest of herself to her family and neighbors, who had all grown weary of spending large portions of their free time searching for the collie-terrier. There was nothing left to do but the honest thing — and that was to write to Jimmy and tell him that his faithful dog had been unable to bear the separation from his master and had run off and gotten himself lost a few days after Jimmy had returned to the front.

But before Colleen could set herself to the terrible task, she received a letter from her husband that left her shaking her head in complete astonishment. A puzzled but elated Jimmy told her that his rugged buddy Prince was there with him on the front lines and sharing a damp berth in the trenches.

In a way that our present levels of conventional knowledge cannot yet comprehend, Prince had somehow negotiated the unfamiliar streets of London, conquered seventy miles of unknown countryside, and sailed across the English Channel. Since the channel constitutes a body of water between England and France no less than twenty miles wide, it is unlikely that Prince swam across. In some way, he obviously managed to hitch a ride on a vessel of some sort that would be docking near the spot in France at which his absentee master was temporarily residing. Once he had managed to get all four of his highly capable paws on

French soil, Prince was next presented with the challenge of making his way sixty miles to the frontline trenches where Jimmy Brown was on duty.

According to the records of this remarkable case, the feisty collie-terrier arrived at the trenches at Armentières at a time when the British line was undergoing a merciless barrage of heavy shellfire from the kaiser's cannons. Ducking bursting shells, dodging erupting earth, and evading deadly gas, Prince was still able to pick up Jimmy's scent among an army of half a million British soldiers. All of his master's trenchmates agreed that there had never been a dog so aptly named and titled as Prince. Once the remarkable story hit the newspapers, the tale of love and devotion of a dog for his owner provided a marvelous uplifting of morale during a time of brutal warfare and inspired those on the British home front to keep the image of a feisty collie–Irish terrier snapping at Kaiser Bill's (Wilhelm II, commander-in-chief of the German armies) trousers seat as a symbol of British dogged determination to triumph.

The wonderful tale of the reunion of Prince and Jimmy in the trenches of France during World War I is one that every dog lover reveres, but when authors seek documentation, they may find that the story is largely anecdotal. Nonetheless, it is an inspiring account of a dog's devotion that might have very well happened exactly as it has been told and retold.

THE SAGA OF HECTOR, THE STOWAWAY DOG: TRUTH IS FAR STRANGER THAN DISNEY'S FICTION

As soon as some readers saw that this entry was about Hector, the Stowaway Dog, they may have begun singing or humming the catchy theme song from *The Ballad of Hector the Stowaway Dog* (1964), a two-part episode of *Walt Disney's Wonderful World of Color.*

"Who is Hector?" asks the song, written by Richard and Robert Sherman, the brothers who wrote the wonderful tunes for *Mary Poppins.*

As so often happens in Hollywood's version of history and real people (and dogs), the answer that the song and the television production gives is a far cry from the true saga of Hector, the stowaway terrier. In the Disney version, Hector is a clever terrier who has a bundle of tricks in his repertoire, and who also has a fortune in jewels sewn into his collar. In the film story, Hector manages to slip aboard a ship carrying a circus troupe to Lisbon.

The true story of Hector, the Stowaway Dog, presents us with one of the most remarkable and well-documented accounts in the annals of dogs-that-came-home tales, for he had to slip aboard a vessel in Vancouver, Washington, and travel to Japan to return to his owner.

While Second Officer Harold Kildall was overseeing the loading of cargo aboard the SS *Hanley* on the morning of April 20, 1922, he spotted a black-and-white terrier walking cautiously up the gangplank. Once on deck, the dog paced about, sniffed at a number of objects, then returned to shore on the Government Dock in Vancouver.

From time to time that day as Kildall went about his various supervisory duties, he noticed the large terrier inspecting four other ships at dock. The seaman was intrigued by the peculiar actions of the dog and by the fact that it seemed to exhibit a genuine sense of purpose in its observation of the vessels. Second Officer Kildall was too busy to pay the terrier any more than occasional attention, for the *Hanley* was getting ready to ship out for Japan.

The next day, when the ship was well on its way to Yokohama, Kildall was astonished to see the big black-and-white terrier walking about on the deck of the *Hanley.* Somehow the dog had managed to stow away aboard the ship.

While a less compassionate captain might have ordered Hector thrown overboard to the sharks and ended the saga of the stowaway dog right then and there, Captain Warner happened to be a dog lover who made the terrier welcome aboard his ship.

Hector soon made it clear that he was willing to work for his passage, for he stood watch with Second Officer Kildall each night. Although the rest of the crew were friendly toward the terrier, Hector remained somewhat aloof toward the common seamen and appeared to be more comfortable at the side of the second officer.

Three weeks later, as the *Hanley* was unloading timber in Yokohama Bay, Kildall observed Hector becoming agitated and restless as their vessel approached the SS *Simaloer,* a Dutch ship that was also unloading wood.

Some time later, when two officers and some crewmen from the *Simaloer* boarded a sampan to begin to move toward the customs landing, Hector began to leap and bark excitedly. As the sampan passed closer to the *Hanley,* the terrier seemed as though he was about to jump overboard and swim toward the boat.

At last one of the passengers of the sampan spotted the big terrier and began to wave his arms and shout. Within a few more moments, Hector was reunited with his master, Willem H. Mante, second officer of the *Simaloer.* Mante explained to Kildall that he and his devoted dog, Hector, had become separated at the Government Dock in Vancouver, and the Dutch ship had left port before he could find his beloved terrier. For Hector to seek and to find his owner, he had to become a stowaway on a ship bound to Japan, a distance of approximately 5,187 nautical miles.

When the case received some circulation among the public, the pioneer parapsychologist Dr. J. B. Rhine of Duke University learned of the remarkable Hector and coined the term "psi-trailing" to describe the extraordinary abilities of animals, particularly dogs, to find their way. Rhine challenged those who attempted to explain Hector's feat of locating his master in another country by ordinary means to answer exactly how Hector had known on which boat to stow away while the ships were docked in Vancouver? And how had Hector known that the *Hanley* was going to Japan and not China, the Hawaiian Islands, or anywhere else?

Captain Kenneth Dodson, USN, saw action in nine major battles during World War II. He had entered the merchant marine immediately after graduating from high school and already had twenty years at sea before the attack on Pearl Harbor in 1941 caused him to enlisted in the navy. After the war, Dodson began producing popular novels about the war, and after his *Away All Boats* (1954) became a successful film, as well as a novel, he became so fascinated by the story of Hector, the stowaway terrier, that he set about checking the accounts of all the witnesses on both vessels. Willem H. Mante told him that as an inveterate dog lover, he had later owned several dogs after the death of the incredible Hector, but none of them could ever take his place. "I'll never forget the faith and friendship of that one-man, one-ship dog, Hector," Mante said.

In Dodson's book, *Hector, the Stowaway Dog* (1958), the naval officer speculates as to what mysterious instinct could have driven the dog's methodical search for the one ship out of so many that would carry him across the ocean to rejoin his beloved master. "Did the character of the *Hanley*'s cargo and perhaps other signs tell him that the *Hanley* was bound for the same destination as his own ship?" Dodson wonders. "Did he then attach himself to the officer whose duties were like his master's? Any answers would only be guesswork."

Kenneth Dodson died at ninety-one in his home in Stanwood, Washington, leaving behind several detailed and accurate portrayals of life at sea, including *Away All Boats, Strangers to the Shore,* and *The China Pirates.*

Interestingly, it is Dodson's book about Hector that served as the inspiration for the Disney show, in which the *Simaloer* becomes a merchant ship headed with a circus troupe to Lisbon, Portugal, rather than a vessel bound for Japan. Hector is a funny dog full of tricks — with over a million dollars in gems sewn into his collar — who sneaks aboard to join the circus. This would not be the first time that Hollywood bought a title of a book and jettisoned the rest.

JOKER FOUND HIS OWNER ON A SECRET MILITARY BASE IN THE PACIFIC

The story of Joker, a cocker spaniel, is in many ways even more remarkable than the legend of Hector, the Stowaway Dog. Somehow, in a journey that defies all reasonable theories, Joker managed to find his way across the Pacific Ocean during World War II and find his owner at a secret military base. As in Hector's case, Joker's story has been completely documented.

During World War II, Army Captain Stanley C. Raye received his orders for overseas duty in the South Pacific. He had no choice other than to leave his cocker spaniel, Joker, with family in his Pittsburg, California, home.

Although he was quite familiar with Raye's family members and he surely knew that he would be treated well in his owner's absence, Joker became terribly despondent. In his doggy mind, it was quite obvious, he and Stanley had something special, a bond without which he could not live. Joker spent two weeks ignoring his food and moping — and then he disappeared.

A few days later, two army doctors reported seeing the stray dog in Oakland, about thirty miles from the Raye home in Pittsburg. But before Joker could be caught, identified, and returned to Captain Raye's family, he had somehow managed to stow away aboard an army transport bound for overseas duty in the South Pacific.

Since this was a military operation, the commanding officers were not as tolerant of a stowaway as Captain Warner had been when he encountered Hector aboard the merchant ship SS *Hanley*. Joker was about to be destroyed when a sympathetic army major volunteered to adopt him and to be responsible for him. It was another example of Joker's remarkable good fortune that the commander granted the major's request.

The army transport made several ports of call, and at each docking Joker was at the helm, sniffing the air and eyeing each seaport inquisitively. It was not until the ship docked at one particular South Pacific island that Joker jumped ship and raced ashore.

Although he was chased and several men attempted to block his course, the cocker spaniel could not be deterred until he was barking joyfully at the feet of a completely astonished Captain Stanley C. Raye.

The major, Joker's adoptive master, was disappointed that the dog had found his true owner, but he could not dispute the cocker spaniel's obvious joy at his reunion with Captain Raye. It was apparent to all those who heard the story of Joker's incredible odyssey that the courageous cocker spaniel had found his true master. Without any hard feelings, the major relinquished his claim on Joker.

How Joker had managed to find Captain

Raye on a military base on a faraway island in the Pacific Ocean remains an unfathomable mystery. Somehow Joker "homed in" on his owner in a secret location in the South Pacific approximately 5,500 nautical miles from his home in Pittsburg, California.

It is unlikely that Captain Raye discussed the details of his orders with Joker. And even if he had been a bit more specific than simply telling his faithful dog that he was going away, what meaning would military jargon describing overseas duty have for a cocker spaniel? For that matter, what meaning would a description of Captain Raye's orders have had for a human civilian? And in point of actual fact, Captain Raye himself may not even have known exactly which South Pacific island would be his base of operations on the night when he said goodbye to Joker.

On January 20, 1958, the Associated Press carried an account of Joker's journey, which surely must be added to the record books as perhaps the ultimate lost-and-found dog miracle. The remarkable Joker lived a rich and full fourteen and one-half years. Until the cocker spaniel died in 1958 in Great Falls, Montana, he and Captain Raye remained inseparable.

The extraordinary travels of Joker to find his human friend truly boggles the mind and causes the thinking person to ask the awesome question of how such things can be. At this time in our research of the mysterious and the unexplained, we cannot even guess what unknown source of knowledge revealed Captain Raye's whereabouts to Joker and guided him successfully on a seemingly impossible journey.

Before his extensive sea voyage, Joker had never been on board a sailing vessel of any kind. What unseen force directed Joker to the Oakland seaport so that he might view the dozens of military vessels and choose to stow away on the very army transport that would take him to Captain Raye? What benign, all-knowing intelligence told Joker which island harbored his master among the many seaports at which the transport docked?

In the next chapter, we shall explore the possibilities that we may always be connected with our beloved pets in a remarkable mind-to-mind linkup that is accessible for all who are willing to accept a somewhat unconventional approach to reality.

CHAPTER 10
THE AMAZING
DOG-HUMAN BOND

DOGS ARE A SIGNIFICANT FORCE
THAT SHAPED HUMANS' SUCCESS
IN THE WORLD

In her book *The Animal Connection: A New Perspective on What Makes Us Human* (2011), Dr. Pat Shipman, adjunct professor of biological anthropology at Penn State University, suggests that our desire to be with animals is a "hugely significant force that has shaped us and been instrumental in our global spread and success in the world." The animal connection, Shipman writes in her article "Creature Contacts" in *New Scientist* (May 28, 2011), creates a trail "that links to three of the most important developments in human evolution: tool-making, language, and domestication." No other species adopts individuals from another species. Who, other than humans, Shipman asks, "would bring a ferocious predator such as a wolf into their home in the hope that thousands of years later it would become a loving family pet?"

The earliest known dog skull, according to the *Journal of Archaeological Science* (Volume 36, page 473), is thirty-two thousand years old, and even if one accepts the earlier date of the domestication of dogs at around seventeen thousand years ago, canines still pre-date any other domesticated animal or plant by about five thousand years.

Here is the great puzzler. One would think that sheep or cattle would have been our species' first domesticated animal. Life in prehistoric times was hard. If the object of domestication was to help create a supply of food at hand to eat, why would humans choose an animal with whom they would have to share the larder that they acquired in dangerous hunting forays? It seems apparent that humans felt they had made a better choice having an animal that would be a dependable ally in tracking other animals, killing them, and then protecting the slain prey from other predators. Better to share with a good hunter than to be hungry during a cold winter.

In his article "Apes, Wolves, and the Trek to Humanity" (*Discovering Archaeology,* March/April 1999), biologist Wolfgang

Schleidt presents a convincing scenario in which *Homo sapiens* or even the earlier *Homo erectus* gathered in small nomadic groups in Northern Europe and joined the wolves in the following of migratory reindeer. It was most fortunate that our lupine partners, with their strength, stamina, keen sense of hearing, and incredible sense of smell, took our slow-moving, clawless, fangless, clumsy species under their guidance. Wolves taught us to be more skillful hunters in tracking prey, and they added the power of their deadly fangs and claws to early humans' sharpened sticks and stone clubs. It can be argued that without their help, our species might not have made it to the Stone Age.

Maude Pionnier-Capitan and her team at the National Museum of History in Paris have uncovered dozens of remains of small dogs at two sites in southern France and another near Paris. The fossils, between 11,500 and 15,500 years old, are contemporaries of much larger ancient dogs whose remains have been found in Russia. The finds of the small canines indicate that domestication of dogs may have occurred independently in various parts of Europe and Asia and much earlier than first supposed. Archaeological and genetic research have also indicated that domestication seems to have occurred almost simultaneously in East Asia and the Middle East, as well as in Europe.

HUMANS AND CANINES EVOLVED TOGETHER

It may be one of humankind's greatest blessings that wolves and their canine descendants were somehow motivated to cooperate with us in our survival and evolution on the planet. Over the past several million years, there have been at least five distinct proto-human species that might have become the masters of the planet that we regard ourselves to be. *Homo sapiens'* closest rival species, *Neanderthal,* with whom we co-existed for many thousands of years, faded gradually into extinction or were absorbed into our species while we grew ever more fruitful and multiplied. It seems not an overstatement to suggest that our species was the one that became dominant because we were the ones who established a symbiotic relationship with canines.

In his book *Evolving Brains* (2000), biologist John Allman of the California Institute of Technology affirms that canines and humans formed a common bond more than 140,000 years ago and evolved together in one of the most successful partnerships ever fashioned. Some genetic studies indicate that the process of domestication that split dogs from wolves date back as far as 100,000 years. An increasing number of archaeological finds present evidence that a relationship between humans and wolves began over 400,000 years ago.

At first, humans got much of the better part of the alliance, for far from being mighty hunters, armed with club and spear, some anthropologists suggest that early humans spent more of their time being hunted. At a presentation at the American Anthropological Association's annual meeting, Donna Hart of the University of Missouri in St. Louis stated that fossil evidence of humans more than a million years old reveals skulls bearing bite marks such as were likely made by saber-toothed cats and leopards. Monkeys and apes, the closest relatives to humans, are still today hunted by 174 kinds of predators, thus supporting a "man, the hunted" theory.

COMPANIONS, GUARDIANS, GUIDES, AND GODS

The entire *canidae* contingent — wolves, coyotes, foxes, and dogs — figured very prominently in the lives of early humans, sometimes as gods, often as demons, always as wise and wily predators, frequently as protectors.

The wolf was a sacred totem and clan symbol for many tribes throughout all of Europe, as well as North America. Many heroes on both sides of the Atlantic claimed ancestry from wolves.

A number of Native American tribes have it in their legends that the first men were created in the shape of wolves. At first these evolving wolves walked on all fours, then, slowly, they began to develop more human features — an occasional toe, a finger, an ear, an eye. As time went by, they evolved two toes, three toes; more fingers; two eyes and ears. Finally, by slow progression, they became perfect men and women. Sadly, though, the legends say, the practice of sitting upright eventually cost them their fine, bushy tails, but now they could always take one from a fox or a wolf to attach to their breeches.

In the folklore of many tribes, the fox was often associated with sorcery and witchcraft, and its image was frequently used by witches as a vehicle into which they projected their spirits when they wished to travel in animal form. As in Europe, the fox became a symbol of wiliness and a crafty kind of wisdom.

The coyote occupies a most unique place in the legends and folklore of the Native Americans, especially for the southwestern tribes. Although he is very often said to have been intimately associated with the Great Mystery in the very act of creation, his wily descendants are both pests and competitors in the tough business of survival in desert country. According to legend, it was the coyote who gave the tribespeople the life-giving gift of fire. He is said to have taught the early people how to grind flour, and he showed them which herbs would bring about which cures. But in spite of his many benevolent acts, Brother Coyote has a most peculiar temperament, and he remains forever a Trickster. While it was he who brought humankind fire, he is also credited for having brought death into the world.

In the majority of Native American tribes, the dog represents fidelity and devotion. The dog symbolizes a friend who is always available when he or she is truly needed. So revered is Brother Dog that many tribes state in their legends that it is one of his kind who waits in the Way of Departed Spirits to assist a recently deceased soul to find its way to the Land of the Grand-parents.

In addition to its role as a guide to the Other Side, many Native American tribes associate the dog with the sun and the moon. Certain folklorists have theorized that such an association may have been due to the dog's well-known penchant for howling at the moon on shadowy, moonlit nights. The dog's connection to the sun may well have derived from what seems to be its instinctive habit of walking around in a small circle before it sits or lies down, and its custom of racing around in circles whenever it has any occasion to be happy or excited. To the early people, a circle was a symbol of the sun, thus ennobling the dog with high status.

The dog was worshiped in Central and South America as well as among the tribes of North America. Interestingly, as the northern tribes often chose the dog as one's totem animal, one's guardian spirit and guide to the world beyond, the southern tribes embraced the concept of the *nahuali,* the animal twin. Quetzalcoatl, the Toletec god of goodness and light and a culture bearer to the central American tribes, had the dog god Xoloti as his *nahauli* and guide.

In ancient Egypt, Anubis, the dog or jackal-headed god, presided over the embalming of the dead and led the spirits of the deceased to the hall of judgment. The Egyptians so revered their dogs that they were buried in family tombs, and family members would shave their heads in mourning at the death of a family dog. In dynastic Egypt, dog mummies were made with the same care and expense given to humans.

Bau, the dog-headed goddess of healing and life, is one of three main deities of the ancient Sumerians. The widespread folk belief that a dog's licking of a wound can promote healing quite likely originates with the legends of the goddess Bau's curative powers. Bau also had seven dog-headed daughters to help carry out her mission of ministering to those who called upon her to banish illness and mend wounds. Later, when Bau was replaced by the goddess Inanna, the new deity had seven hunting dogs. Royal inscriptions in Sumeria proclaim that members of royalty and honored military figures were known as *ur-sag,* "top dog."

The pantheon of the Greek and Roman gods and goddesses included Leto, the mother of Apollo and Artemis (Diana), who took the form of a wolf. Both Leto and Artemis were accompanied by wolves, and Artemis was known as the wolf goddess. The wolf was also Apollo's sacred animal.

Hecate, the goddess of death, was sometimes depicted with a dog's head, and Cerberus, the three-headed dog, guarded the entrance to Hades, the underworld. The she-wolf who suckled Romulus and Remus became the emblem of Rome.

In Persia, dogs were believed to be able to protect the soul from evil spirits; when a person was dying, a dog was stationed by his or her bedside to keep away the evil spirits who hovered near newly released souls.

Odin/Woden, the chief Norse deity, relied on two wolves, Freki and Geri, as his guides, guardians, and companions. Odin's death is predicted to occur when Fenrir, the great wolf of the apocalypse, is set free to ravage the earth. Hel, the underworld, is guarded by the huge dog Garm and his pack of wolves and dogs.

In ancient Vedic literature, Indra has Sarama, his faithful female dog, as his companion and messenger, whose two sons, the Sarameyas, became the messengers and companions of Yama, the lord of death.

Since at least the Han Dynasty (206 BCE–220 CE), dogs in China were given royal status. The Emperor Ling Ti (156–189 CE) gave royal titles to his palace dogs, considering them as imperial guards and viceroys.

In both Tibet and China, lion dog statues served as sacred guardians of temples.

Tibetans believe that dogs are closest to humans on the spiritual ladder of reincarnation. Dogs, in their next incarnations, will be humans. High lamas often reincarnate as dogs to enter the cycle of rebirth on a higher rung.

In a number of Byzantine depictions, St. Christopher, the venerated saint of travelers, has the head of a dog. While the mother of the future St. Dominic was pregnant with her son, she had a vivid dream of a dog holding a torch in his mouth that would set the earth on fire. Dominic went on to found the Dominican order — in Latin, Dominicanus, "dog of the Lord."

The brightest star in the heavens, Sirius, commonly known as the dog star, is the largest body in the constellation of Canis Major, the Big Dog in the night sky that looks over the Earth at night.

THE DOG'S BRAIN
CONTINUES TO EVOLVE

In December 2005, biologists at the Broad Institute in Cambridge, Massachusetts, released information that they had decoded the dog genome to a high degree of accuracy, thereby meshing into the evolutionary history of *Canis familiaris* and its companion species, *Homo sapiens.* Nicholas Wade, reporting on the findings for *The New York Times* (December 7, 2005), stated that "genes for brain function seem to have evolved faster than others in both dogs and people. This could be because social animals need extra computing power to recognize one another and predict one another's behavior."

And speaking of the dog's evolving brain, who do you think is smarter — your canine puppy or a wolf puppy? Is the wolf, hailed by Native American tribes as the Great Teacher, the more intelligent? The wolf must live in the wilderness against incredible odds and survive by its wits and cunning. Or is your congenial puppy, living large by your side, warm and well-fed in your home, the more intelligent of the two cousins?

Since 1997, research fellow Adam Miklosi has been studying the cognitive abilities of man's best friend in Budapest, Hungary, at Eotvos Lorand University's Department of Ethology. The experiments have revealed that dogs have far greater mental capabilities than scientists had previously thought. The cumulative evidence demonstrates that dogs' intelligence manifests in their relationships with people and that dogs may make better cognitive study subjects than primates.

Until recent tests and studies, perhaps the majority of scientists believed that the process of domestication over the centuries had dulled dogs' intelligence. Studies conducted in the early 1980s revealed that wolves, from which dogs probably descended, could unlock a gate after watching a human do it once, while dogs remained apparently baffled by the process, even after observing the actions repeatedly.

The conclusions drawn from the "unlocking the gate" tests were never accepted well by Vilmos Csanyi, the retired head of Adam Miklosi's department. Csanyi, a dog owner, suspected the dogs used in the tests were awaiting their owner's permission to open the gate. Well-trained dogs, always eager to please and keep harmony at all costs, would regard the opening of a gate as a violation of their master's rules.

In 1997, Csanyi and his colleagues at Eotvos Lorand University's Department of Ethology tested twenty-eight dogs of various ages, breeds, and degrees of bonding to their owners to see if the domesticated pooches could learn to obtain cuts of meat on the other side of a fence by pulling on the handles of dishes while their owners were present. Dogs who enjoyed a close bond with their owners did not do as well in this test as outdoor, ownerless dogs. But when the dogs' owners were permitted to give their obedient canine companions verbal permission to fetch the meat, the gap between the groups of dogs vanished.

Dogs excel at imitating people. "We thought it would be very difficult for dogs to imitate humans," Csanyi said to journalist Colin Woodard, writing in *The Christian Science Monitor* ("Why Your Dog Is Smarter than a Wolf," October 26, 2005). "Chimps have great difficulty doing so, even with their larger brains. But it turns out [dogs] love to do it. This is not a little thing, because they must pay attention to the person's actions, remember them, and then apply them to their own body."

And Csanyi and his colleagues demonstrated in experiment after experiment that even young puppies have got "smarts." According to Csanyi, "Dogs' unusual ability and motivation to observe, imitate, and communicate with people appears to be with them from birth."

In a two-year experiment, graduate students in the ethology department were given either a wolf cub or a puppy to raise. They gave the two canines equal attention, care, and coddling, but in a series of tests, at crucial aspects of the experiments, the wolf cubs seemed often to ignore their human caregivers while the puppies would seek to work with their partners, turning to them for assistance or clues. In some tests, the puppies appeared to understand that the problem would more easily be solved by canine-human cooperation.

In Csanyi's interpretation of the experiments, dogs have acquired an innate ability to pay attention to people and have learned to communicate and work with them. This is a skill of interspecies communication that is one that wolves don't assume even when raised from birth to learn it.

Dogs are "very motivated to cooperate with and behave like people," says Csanyi. "That's why dogs can do things no other animal can do."

Brains of Dogs and Humans Are "Hardwired" for Each Other

In the September 23, 2011, issue of *Psychology Today,* Lee Charles Kelley theorizes that (1) there is a part of the human brain that is designed to make us pay attention to all animals, particularly dogs; (2) dogs may have a similar cognitive function hardwired into their brains that makes them pay special attention to humans, (3) the human brain and dog brain may sometimes act in concert.

Dr. Pat Shipman discloses that new findings by a team of neurobiologists strongly supports the theory that a connection between humans and dogs is extremely important and "very inheritable." The right amygdala of the human brain appears to be dedicated specifically to the recognition of the shapes and movements of animals, and nothing else. Such a form of pattern recognition releases dopamine, making the human observer feel at ease.

In the August 2010 issue of *Current Anthropology,* Shipman names the human-animal connection as the first phase in what eventually became the domestication process. This phase, she posits, took place over 2.5 million years ago and was quite likely based on the shared hunting patterns between our ancestors and wolves.

Lee Charles Kelley points out that if the ancestors of dogs and humans share such a long history, it would seem logical that the right amygdala in the human brain would pay special attention to the shapes and movements of dogs, the most social, and also the most aggressive, animal on the planet. Kelley also suggests that dogs may also have a humanoid template hardwired into the right amygdala of their brains.

ARE DOGS "PRACTICALLY" HUMAN?

David Blouin, cultural sociologist at Indiana University at South Bend, told Stephanie Pappas (*Live Science,* August 15, 2010) that his research indicated three types of dog and pet owners. There are the Dominionists, who do not mistreat their dogs and are generally fond of them, but who regard them primarily not as companions, but as useful animals. The Humanists become extremely close to their dogs and believe that they are practically human. The Protectionists do not see dogs as nearly human, but they recognize that humans do have a responsibility to help and to protect another species. People who live in rural areas are more likely to be Dominionists while city dwellers are slightly more likely to hold Humanists views toward their dogs.

It seems likely that every dog lover who fits the Humanist category has, on some occasion or other, been criticized by the Dominionists and others for treating their dog as if it were human. While the negative comments may range from gentle teasing to scientific or religious admonishment to maintain a distance between a mere animal and a human being, passionate dog owners are often reminded that dogs cannot experience emotions or a range of intelligence comparable to those of humans.

Dr. Stanley Coren, a widely respected authority on dogs and the author of such books as *Why Does My Dog Act That Way?*, *Born to Bark*, and *The Intelligence of Dogs*, poses the question "Is Anthropomorphism a Sin? Thinking About Dogs as if They Were People" and provides an excellent response in *Psychology Today* (November 21, 2011).

During a recent talk to an audience of scientists and university professors, Dr. Coren was chided by a well-known animal researcher for excessive "anthropomorphizing" when he referred to the "personality" of dogs and the fact that they can experience such emotions as love and disgust. To regard dogs as if they are "four-footed people in fur coats" is a cardinal sin to those who study dogs scientifically.

Coren admits that he tried early in his research to be scientifically dispassionate about animals, but he couldn't help noticing that those individuals who actually worked with and cared for animals described their behaviors with "the same kind of intuition that we normally use when we observe the behavior of people . . . [describing] one animal as having a 'dominant personality,' another as being 'nervous,' another was considered to be a 'friendly beast'; still another was 'shy' and there was even one that they claimed was 'bashful.' These were clearly anthropomorphic statements which suggested that, like people, the animals had distinct and individual personalities, and that you could use their personalities to predict the animals' future behaviors."

Drawing upon the research that has accumulated in the past twenty years, Coren feels justified in speaking about dogs in such "anthropomorphic" terms. "Research suggests that the mind of a dog has much the same mental abilities and is roughly equivalent to the mind of a human child aged two to two and a half years of age," he points out. "This means that a bit of anthropomorphizing about dogs in the same way we think about humans actually turns out to be useful. . . . If we accept the fact that dogs, like toddlers, have personalities, in the sense that they also have consistent predispositions to act in certain ways, then we can use the same kind of thinking that we use with people to predict canine behaviors. This is not anthropomorphism, it is simply common sense that recognizes those similarities that exist between the mind of a person and the mind of a dog."

In other studies, Coren has estimated that the average dog has a "vocabulary" of 165 words, including signals. The "super dogs," those in the top 20 percent of dog intelligence, can learn 250 words.

Coren has concluded that dogs can learn the location of specially valued items, such as treats and toys, better routes in the environment, such as the fastest way to a favorite chair, how to operate door latches and other simple mechanisms, and the meaning of symbolic words and concepts by listening to people speak and watching their actions. During play, Coren commented, dogs are capable of deliberately attempting to deceive other dogs and people in order to obtain rewards. And, Coren, concluded, dogs are nearly as successful in deceiving humans as humans are in deceiving dogs.

SHIRLEY MACLAINE HAS NO PROBLEM "ANTHROPOMORPHIZING" TERRY, HER RAT TERRIER

The always delightful and provocative award-winning actress-singer-dancer-author Shirley MacLaine has absolutely no problem with anyone accusing her of "anthropo-morphizing" her relationship with her dog, Terry. In her book *Out on a Leash* (2003), she openly shares the lessons that she has learned from Terry, the little rat terrier who is her constant companion, traveling every-where with her, bringing her love, peace, and joy.

"Terry has taught me simplicity," she told Serene Conneeley of *New Idea,* a national weekly magazine. "She has completely changed my priorities. . . . She doesn't have to have any plan, so I am learning to live without a plan, too. Of course when I go to work, I'm very efficient, and a strong work ethic is my top priority. But with Terry, the priority is to just allow whatever happens to happen, good and bad."

Although Shirley has traveled the world and met royalty, heads of governments, spiritual teachers, actors, and musicians, she commented that she had never met anyone who had taught her as much about the world or herself as Terry has. "There have been many different people in my life, but with the relationships we have with humans — family, lovers, friends, teachers, whoever — there is always some hidden agenda. I don't have an agenda with Terry. I have no expectations with her. . . . She is quite capable of being her own independent crusader."

Terry's profound, innate sophistication of simplicity has taught Shirley to live more that way, as well as to be less judgmental of others.

The bestselling author and popular actress has encountered many very intelligent and wise individuals in her life, but Shirley is most impressed by the wisdom that animals possess, and she is convinced that if we open our hearts and minds to them, we can learn a great deal from them. "They live with another understanding of reality," she said. "What about a [dog] that can find its way home from four thousand miles?"

SAM THE DACHSHUND AND TEDDY CROCKARELL

The story of Teddy Crockarell and Sam illustrates most profoundly the ancient, amazing, and almost supernatural dog-human bond.

Teddy Crockarell wanted to take no chances with his beloved dachshund, Sam, leaving the yard unescorted, so he had an underground electric fence installed and placed a collar sensitive to the line around Sam's little neck. If Sam should happen to wander outside of the invisible fence line, he would receive a slight shock which would warn him to retreat.

At two and a half years old, Sam would never knowingly stray from the confines of house and lawn. Sam was devoted to Teddy, and the two souls seemed connected on so many levels.

On Monday, April 7, 2008, Teddy Crockarell succumbed to the cancer which he had valiantly been fighting.

When the family returned home from the hospital, the first thing they noticed was that Sam was not waiting for them in the yard. Sam had run away.

Teddy's wife, Marcene, said that Sam had never ignored the warning shock that he would receive from the electric fence. Sam had never left home by himself.

The family called for Sam and vigorously searched the neighborhood, but it soon became apparent that the little dachshund had left them. Sam's disappearance added to the family's grief, knowing how much Teddy had loved his little dog.

Two and a half days later, the family arrived at a church six miles away for Teddy Crockerell's funeral.

There, sitting by the doors waiting for them, was Sam, shivering and shaking.

Marcene told Amy Napier Viteri of

WKRN-TV in Nashville that the entire family just "lost it." One by one, they all picked him up and hugged him. Sam had never been at the church before. Yet, there he was, waiting for the rest of them to join him in honoring the memory of Teddy.

Howard, Teddy's and Marcene's son-in-law, commented that Sam had walked those six miles on his little dachshund legs looking for Papa.

Somehow Sam had known the moment that Teddy had died and had run away to grieve in private.

Somehow Sam knew when and where the funeral service would be held and had walked there to join the family in their sorrow.

As many thoughtful individuals have asked, what has our species ever done to deserve the devotion and unconditional love of dogs?

CHAPTER 11
CAN OUR DOGS READ OUR MINDS? CAN WE READ THEIRS?

Many dog owners insist that they have a telepathic linkup with their beloved canines and that they are able to communicate with their pet as if they are of one mind. If there is a totality that envelops all beings, then telepathy — mind-to-mind communication — would be easy to accomplish if the minds of all living creatures were somehow united in a great universal mind pool.

DID HER MIND-TO-MIND CONNECTION WITH DICK SAVE BELVA'S LIFE?

A correspondent who wishes to be known only as Dick told us of an incredible psychic linkup that he believed saved his dog's life.

Dick was just returning from a four-day out-of-town business trip. He needed to head directly for his office, but on the way he called his daughter, Erin, to see when it would be convenient for him to swing by her place and pick up Belva, his ten-year-old female beagle. Erin had been dogsitting for him while he was away on business.

"When her answering machine came on, I decided that she must be working a bit late or had stopped off somewhere on her way home," Dick told us. "I left a message that I was home, that I had to swing by the office, but I would be at her place to pick up Belva no later than six. If that was not all right, she should call me."

Dick was nearly to his office when he began to receive strange images in his head. He was suddenly filled with an overwhelming sense of dread and fear, as if something terrible were about to happen.

Dick pulled into an empty space in a supermarket parking lot and called his office to see if some crisis situation awaited him. His secretary welcomed him back and said everything was fine. Just the ordinary stack of mail that had piled up during his absence.

"The images were becoming darker and more threatening," Dick told us. "Somehow it was as if another intelligence took control of me. I backed the car out of the parking space, left the lot, and headed back into traffic — in the opposite direction from my office."

Dick drove all the way across town without having any idea of where he was going. It was only when he pulled up in front of the local Humane Society that he realized where he was and what he was doing there. Somehow he knew that his precious Belva was in the pound and was about to be put to death.

For an instant, Dick's rational mind attempted to argue with him, to calm him down with an admonition of how ridiculously impossible such a thought was. Belva was safely in the care of Erin. At that very moment, she was probably having a snack of those little nut-flavored dog bones that she loved.

"It is difficult to explain," Dick said, "but somehow I *knew* that Belva was in the pound, that she was about to be put down, and that she had been crying out to me to come to save her. There was no thinking involved. It was a *knowing.*"

Once inside the building, it took Dick another fifteen minutes to explain to those in charge why he was there.

"I still shudder at the thought," he recalled, "but the people on duty told me that if I had been another hour later, it would have been too late. Belva had been there unclaimed without dog tags for seventy-two hours. The new rules were strict. Seventy-two hours was the cutoff time for someone to reclaim a dog. Belva was already set to be put to sleep within the hour. I know that she sent me a cry for help. She knew that she was going to die, and she telepathically called out to me."

Later that evening, Dick got the full story from his daughter. One day she had come home from work and discovered that Belva was gone. Since she and her father each had keys to one another's apartments, she thought that he must have come back from his business trip earlier than expected and picked up his dog. In actuality, Belva had somehow managed to slip out of the apartment and had taken to the streets.

"Erin didn't think too much of it that I didn't call her," Dick said. "She knew that I would have lots of work at the office to catch up on and thought that I would get together with her on the weekend."

Belva was a complete stranger to running loose on the streets. It was anyone's guess about what happened to her dog tags. What is known for certain is that the dogcatchers picked her up and took her to the pound.

Because the Humane Society in Dick's city only keeps unclaimed, untagged dogs for seventy-two hours, Belva's time was running out very fast when Dick's airplane landed at the airport. If he had ignored those strange images and feelings that besieged him and continued on to his office, his precious Belva would have been put to death.

Dick told us that he will never be able to explain what strange kind of intelligence took control of him and made him drive across the city to the Humane Society, but he sincerely believes that it was as if Belva's cry for help had become one with his entire being and was giving him directions that he simply had to follow.

"If I had shaken these feelings off with my rational mind and had gone on to the office, believing Belva to be safe in Erin's apartment, Belva would have been put to sleep," Dick concluded. "I shall always believe that our minds, our very souls, made telepathic contact that day and saved Belva's life."

CAN OUR DOGS READ OUR MINDS?

In the June 4, 2011, issue of *Learning & Behavior,* Monique A. R. Udell, Nicole R. Dorey, and Clive D. L. Wynne (Department of Psychology, University of Florida) published their study "Can Your Dog Read Your Mind? Understanding the Causes of Canine

Perspective Taking," in which they state that instances of apparent "canine telepathy" rely upon hyper-awareness of the senses. Their studies also appear to demonstrate that dogs, as well as their living ancestors, wolves, are seemingly hardwired with the ability to read a human's mental states.

Focusing on the domestic dog, the study notes that *canis lupus familiaris* has shown the capability of "responding to human body language, verbal commands, and attentional states to a degree that has equaled, or in some cases surpassed, our closest primate relatives, chimpanzees." Monique Udell and her team found even more astounding the "repeated successful demonstrations of theory-of-mind abilities in dogs."

For years a heated debate has been conducted by psychologists of animal behavior as to whether dogs have a consciousness similar to humans or whether they simply act in response to environmental stimulation without conscious thought. We humans recognize that others of our species may have thoughts, insights, and observations different from our own. Do dogs have a similar ability to recognize that we are seeing the world differently than the one that they perceive through their senses? In simplistic terms, we observe our dog and wonder what he is thinking. Does our dog observe us and wonder what *we* are thinking?

Longtime and observant dog owners will argue that dogs most certainly do have consciousness, a sense of self, and an awareness that humans provide all sorts of clues as to what they are thinking. Dogs are so good at observing our slightest moves, moods, and facial expressions that it does seem that on occasion they can read our minds. At the very least, it seems that they do have a theory of mind and that they are always trying to figure out what we are thinking so that they might please us.

Those of us who have owned a dog for any period of time have recognized how well our canine companion senses our happiness, headaches, fatigue, or illnesses, even before we consciously display any signs of distress. During good times or bad times, they are there by our sides, indicating by their whining, barking, or jumping that they want to do anything they can to help us celebrate or to get us through the problem.

Udell and her fellow researchers state that the results of their study "suggest that dogs' ability to follow human actions stems from a willingness to accept humans as social companions, combined with conditioning to follow the limbs and actions of humans to acquire reinforcement. The type of attentional clues, the context in which the command is presented, and previous experience are all important."

INTERSPECIES COMMUNICATORS

After several hundred thousand years as intimate partners on a very rugged and hazardous evolutionary path, it should come as no surprise that there are certain men and women who believe that their rapport with dogs is so powerful that they are able literally to speak to the canines, as well as other animals, around them.

On February 26, 2000, Burl Burlingame of the *Honolulu Star Bulletin* spoke with Bill Northern, who claimed that he could speak with the animals, just like Dr. Dolittle in the popular series of children's books.

In summarizing the various attitudes that different types of pets might hold toward their owners, Northern said, "Horses think we're around to serve them. If you're late bringing their food, a horse thinks, What's the matter with that so-and-so? And dogs think, What did I do wrong to deserve a late meal? Dogs will go out of their way not to hurt your feelings. And cats will think, Dinner's late. I better go kill something!"

Dr. Pauline Yap of Companion Animal Hospital in Kailua, Hawaii, commented that certain observations made by Northern could be attributed to general observations that would be apparent to anyone who spent a great deal of time around animals. There are, Dr. Yap pointed out, certain "clichés about horse and dog and cat behavior [that are] generally accurate for most animals."

But can some people truly "talk" to animals? Are there genuine "dog whisperers" among us?

In response to a similar query from journalist Burl Burlingame, Dr. Yap acknowledged that it was "more of a philosophical question than a scientific or medical one," but she replied further that ". . . it's certainly true that some people — particularly those who grew up around animals — instinctively know how to behave to put an animal at ease. It's a physical language. I see this regularly with some people. Animals just react well to them."

And, Dr. Yap emphasized, animals read people very well. "They're very sensitive to our moods, our vibes. I knew from childhood, for example, that I had a natural affinity for animals. It wasn't something I learned — it was natural."

Dr. Halina Zaleski of the University of Hawaii Animal Sciences Department is also quoted by Burlingame as observing that such nonverbal communication is a two-way street, but animals appear to be better at "speaking" it than most humans.

"Animals are generally sensitive to people's moods and feelings," Dr. Zaleski said, "but some people have a much better instant rapport with animals than others — just like some people are good with kids and others aren't."

Penelope Smith of Point Reyes, California, author of *Animals . . . Our Return to Wholeness,* believes that everyone was born with the ability to communicate telepathically with animals.

"This ability is carefully squeezed out of us when we are children," Smith said. "Telepathy is considered something weird or strange, but in actual fact, it is the universal language."

As one who has communicated with animals all of her life, Smith stated that one must first learn how to quiet the mind. "Once your mind is open and receptive, the images and impressions of what the animal is thinking and feeling will come through. All beings are quite capable of understanding another being without opening their mouths. The whole secret of what I do is to listen to them."

It would appear that a great number of open-minded scientists acknowledge in one way or another that there is something going on between humans and animals on an unconscious, intuitive level. Perhaps most of these doctors and researchers would cautiously point out that a number of alleged instances of human-animal communication can be explained by ordinary sensory clues that the pet has learned to identify, but we feel quite certain that a good many scientists would agree with Dr. Larry Dossey's provocative assertions in his book *Recovering the Soul: A Scientific and Spiritual Search* that there may well be a "non-local, universal mind" that connects all living creatures on Earth.

Dr. Dossey states that "it makes good biological sense that a non-local, psychological communion might have evolved between humans and animals as an asset to survival."

If such communion does exist, then all the stories of dogs returning home to their owners and accounts of telepathic exchanges between humans and their canine companions become, in the words of Dr. Dossey, "more than amusing parlor tales." Such stories, indeed, become ". . . indicators that nature in its wisdom would, in fact, have designed a mind that envelops all creatures great and small."

A PSYCHIC LOCATED MISSING JACK RUSSELL TERRIER

In May 2008, Nikki Newcombe was becoming desperate. Her Jack Russell terrier, Marmite, had been missing for a week in the West Midlands near Walsall, England. She and her daughter had done all the "logical" things that one does when a dog goes missing, so she decided to resort to other more unconventional means to find Marmite.

Newcombe had heard of a psychic named Pea Horsley, who stated that she had the ability to communicate telepathically with dogs or any other species of animal. Although Horsley was in London, over a hundred miles from the area, she said that she was able to see mental pictures of Marmite's location. The terrier, she said, was wedged in a human-made concrete hole with water at the bottom. The psychic also described the route that Marmite had taken when he disappeared.

According to the *Daily Mail* (May 12, 2008), Nikki Newcombe followed the details that Horsley had provided and went to the locks of a canal that was no longer in use. The canal was about a mile from her home, but the location seemed to fit the description given by the psychic.

After a week of fruitless searching, within an hour of following Horsley's directions, Newcombe and her daughter found Marmite wedged in a shaft below a narrow section of the sluice gate. As soon as he heard their voices, he began to bark and to jump excitedly up and down. It was obvious that Marmite was eager to be freed from his dark, cold prison.

They immediately called the fire department and asked for help. A crew arrived from the fire department and lowered Marmite's basket into the chamber inside the canal sluice gate. The men, together with Nikki Newcombe, coaxed the terrier into getting inside. Within minutes, the despair that had begun a week ago had ended with a joyous reunion.

Ms. Newcombe and her daughter considered Pea Horsley's ability to connect with Marmite in his damp dungeon nothing short of a miracle and declared that they have truly become believers in the world of psychic phenomena.

Horsley explained that once she had achieved a psychic attunement with

Marmite, she could sense that he was still alive and could see clearly exactly where he was trapped. It was this mental connection that allowed her to describe a precise route that Nikki Newcombe could follow to reclaim her beloved Marmite.

GAYLE NASTASI TUNES IN ON LOST MATTIE AND HELPS BRING HER HOME TO HER OWNERS

Gayle Nastasi has worked professionally in the animal-care field since the early 1980s and she has also received training in the fields of alternative medicine and psychic studies. She is in great demand for her unique talents, and she often works on several lost pet cases at the same time.

In her experience with animals on the psychic or mental level, she has found that animals rarely think in words or in the same kind of thought concepts that humans do. When Gayle makes a telepathic linkup with a dog, she receives a hodgepodge of impressions. She may receive images, emotions, and even such physical or sensory input as smells and sounds. What she does, she explained, is to try to put all the pieces of input together and bring them some cohesive order in which to discuss them with the animal's owner. Thus employing such a

299

technique, it is her hope that together they may interpret the seemingly scattered impressions and make sense of them.

We are pleased to present the following account that Gayle shared with us in which she was able to help locate a lost dog that was very dear to her two owners.

On October 27, 2007, Debbie Bowman and her housemate, Pat Box, who live in the Yeoman Lake community of northeastern Georgia, were walking their four dogs — Callie, Macy, and Murphy, purebred golden retrievers, and little Mattie, a mixed breed, who, in spite of her much smaller size, ruled the pack. Debbie had acquired Mattie from the White County Animal Shelter, and, at once, Mattie had become the dominant dog energy in the house.

Debbie strongly emphasized that all of their dogs had collars and tags, but on this particular Saturday, she and Pat were letting them run off leash in the woods. It was growing dark, and the owners felt a brisk run before returning home would let the dogs release pent-up energy.

Bold Mattie took off ahead of the three retrievers. Debbie and Pat heard Mattie release a yelp, and they both assumed that she had spotted a deer and had taken off after it. Because it was becoming dark, neither of them saw exactly in which direction Mattie had headed.

And then, almost at once it seemed, it was very dark. And Mattie had not returned with Callie, Murphy, and Macy.

Debbie and Pat shouted for her to come back to them, but their desperate calls were in vain. They were forced to return home without Mattie.

The next day, with no Mattie scratching at the door or lying asleep on their doorstep, Debbie Bowman and Pat Box set to the task of making flyers that they would soon post all around the Yeoman Lake and Army's Creek area, as well as the Clarkesville Veterinary Hospital area. They also placed signs in a number of local businesses.

Later, completely unable simply to sit and wait for someone to spot Mattie, Debbie and Pat enlisted the help of their friends and neighbors to conduct a canvass of the area.

It seemed impossible that Mattie had disappeared within the range of their hearing but just out of their sight on Saturday. And, then, even more incredible, another day had passed — and still no sign of Mattie.

But on Tuesday, October 30, they received a telephone call from someone who thought she may have seen Mattie in the Sweetwater subdivision off Highway 255 Alternate. Bowman and Box made a quick drive to the area and brought some friends to help them scour the neighborhood, but no sign of Mattie was to be found.

It was about that time that a friend named Molly Moncure suggested that the two call a psychic named Gayle Nastasi, who had helped her find her missing German shepherd a few years earlier. Even though Nastasi wasn't familiar with northeastern Georgia, she had located Molly's dog in Habersham County.

Debbie Bowman decided to call Nastasi. She had received a report on October 31 that a woman had spotted Mattie on Amy's Creek Church Road. Four days had already passed with Mattie lost and confused. She knew that they needed to find her soon, before something dreadful happened to her.

Nastasi's very first impression of Mattie was that she was a very talkative little female, always busy and very smart.

Debbie and Pat agreed that the psychic had definitely made contact with their absent Mattie.

Psychically, Mattie told Nastasi that her feet hurt.

Debbie and Pat were upset about Mattie's

pain, but Gayle told them that Mattie's complaint about her feet was a good thing. Often, when animals did not report any pain, it could mean that they were dead.

Through Gayle Nastasi's psychic attunement, Mattie told Debbie and Pat that on the day that she disappeared she saw a large cat and took off after it. Suddenly it had turned around and hissed at her. This reversal of roles in the chase had frightened Mattie and made her lose her bearings. Then, in addition to the fright caused by the big cat's aggression, Mattie had run up a hill onto the road and almost been hit by a car.

There was no question, Gayle said as gently as possible, that Mattie was frightened and wanted to come home. Mattie said that she was hiding in some bushes and that she was very cold. She was near water and up a hill in some woods. She wanted to show herself to people, but she was afraid of them.

Under Gayle Nastasi's questioning, Mattie said that she had seen a woman pushing a child on a swing. The little dog admitted that she was somewhat afraid of children.

Nastasi told Mattie that she should show herself to women such as those who came to push little children on swings.

Mattie expressed her reluctance, stating that she preferred to hide and that she had dug herself a depression in the earth in which to hide from predators.

After this exchange, the psychic informed Debbie Bowman that she was going to employ what she believed to be the spirit energy of a white saluki named Yoda, who had been one of Nastasi's own pets before it died in 1993. The saluki, known as the royal dog of Egypt, is one of the oldest known breeds. Yoda, she assured Debbie and Pat, had guided many other lost pets back to their owners' homes. Yoda, she explained further, would instruct Mattie to seek out and to follow the white light that was shining above Debbie's and Pat's house.

After the session was concluded, Debbie and Pat decided that they would attempt to pinpoint the various landmarks that Gayle Nastasi had revealed through her psychic contact with Mattie. They called some friends and neighbors and set out into the night, searching and calling for Mattie.

After a fruitless two hours, with voices growing hoarse from shouting and legs aching from negotiating the area where they had hoped Mattie might be, the search was abandoned.

On Thursday, November 1, Debbie Bowman and Pat Box contacted Gayle Nastasi and asked her to see if Mattie could provide any clearer information about the place where she was hiding.

After she emerged from a meditative state in which she communicated with Mattie, Gayle learned that the little dog had found herself in some deep mud when she went to get a drink. She had seen a man sitting in a truck and she tried to summon the courage to approach him, but she had instead become fearful and ran away.

According to Nastasi, Mattie had described playground swings, a cement culvert, a fire hydrant, and sidewalks. At times, Mattie seemed to be describing some kind of school or business with a parking lot.

Bowman and Box were puzzled by these descriptions because sidewalks were not common in northeastern Georgia. Perhaps Mattie was confusing well-worn walking paths with sidewalks.

The days and nights were growing colder, and Debbie and Pat became increasingly concerned about Mattie's well-being. Where could she be?

They continued to receive telephone calls from individuals who believed that they had sighted Mattie. Unfortunately, they all proved to be false alarms, but at least they demonstrated to Debbie and Pat that people were still concerned about their Mattie and that they were keeping her in their thoughts and prayers.

On November 2, weather forecasters predicted that temperatures would dip down into the high thirties that night. Debbie and Pat were painfully aware that it was imperative that Mattie be someplace warm that night.

When they e-mailed Gayle Nastasi for some words of encouragement, she told them that Mattie had sought refuge in an old building deep in the woods. She could see a number of old cars behind a fence, and she was able to smell a chicken house.

Gayle said that Mattie was having a problem trusting Yoda, the spirit dog that the psychic had sent to help guide Mattie home. However, Gayle reassured Debbie and Pat that Mattie still trusted her and would stay in communication with her.

Gayle Nastasi told us that she makes a practice of making an encouraging connection or reconnection with lost animals before she falls asleep at night. In reflecting on the case of Mattie later on January 20, 2008, Gayle said that at this point in the psychic search, she was working with a number of lost animals for a number of very concerned owners.

"Working on so many cases at once was becoming a bit draining, so I shifted to positive visualization and asked Debbie Bowman and Pat Box to join me in generating the images," she said. "Such visualizations consist of forming clear images of seeing Mattie coming home, being in their arms, feeling the joy of their love. The purpose of these visualizations is to build a reality through thoughts and faith in which Mattie would in actuality come home."

On November 4, there was a message on Debbie Bowman's cell phone from a Debbie S., who had read about Mattie in the *Northeast Georgian* and who believed that she had found the missing dog. Debbie S. left her telephone number and said that she was from Riverwilde.

Debbie Bowman and Pat Box had never heard of Riverwilde. A friend told them that it was a subdivision of Clarkesville and was about ten miles away. The friend also told them that there was a technical college in Riverwilde.

Debbie and Pat decided not to get their hopes up. They agreed that there was no way that little Mattie could have wandered ten miles away from home.

Although Debbie S. didn't answer their

call, the two housemates decided to drive to Riverwilde and just survey the area while they waited for Debbie S. to return their message.

After arriving in the subdivision and driving around a bit, they found themselves in a parking lot behind the automotive school.

And there it all was. Everything that Mattie had described through Gayle Nastasi was spread out before them.

There was a concrete reservoir, a water tower, and lots of old cars behind a chain-link fence. Next to the college there was a day care center with swings in the play area. And there were many sidewalks around the college.

Debbie Bowman admitted later to writer Amber Allen that at this point she and Pat started to get "freaked out."

When they connected with Debbie S. and her husband, William, and got their address, they found them waiting in their driveway with Mattie on a leash. Mattie was overjoyed when she spotted Debbie and Pat, and the two women rushed forward to embrace Mattie, William, Debbie, and their sons.

On Saturday night, November 3, William and Debbie had let one of their two dogs outside and were surprised to hear him barking at something. When William investigated, he found a beautiful little dog hiding behind the garbage cans. Debbie was convinced that it was the missing dog that she had been reading about in the newspaper. They fed her, kept her in the garage overnight, and called Debbie Bowman in the morning. All the while, they were praying that this was the dog for which Debbie Bowman and Pat Box had been searching.

Gayle Nastasi wept when she was informed that Mattie had come home. The little dog had at last worked up the courage to approach strangers and ask for help. And it turned out that William and Debbie were, indeed, the perfect ones with whom to seek solace.

Mattie's three pals, Macy, Callie, and Murphy, were delighted to have her back in the fold. Mattie had lost some weight from her ordeal and would need some good meals to bring her back to trim, and she headed to her warm bed next to the woodburning stove to get the chill out of her bones.

We are grateful to Gayle Nastasi for bringing this marvelous lost-and-found dog miracle story to our attention. Writer Amber Allen was inspired by the saga of Mattie to write a two-part story in the *Northeast Georgian* on December 20 and 27, 2007.

Nastasi soberly reminded us that not all lost-and-found dog stories have happy endings. The loss of a dog can bring forth great emotions and can be so distracting that they block the flow of communication between an animal communicator and the dog. While Debbie and Pat were very concerned and worried about Mattie, Nastasi said, they were able to remain calm and work with her through the experience.

Love is such a powerful emotion, Nastasi said, and anyone who does not believe that it can exist strongly between humans and animals is to be pitied.

CAN YOUR DOG READ YOUR MIND? DO YOU WANT TO READ HIS?

Certainly the accounts in this chapter appear to support Dr. Larry Dossey's concept of the "non-local mind." If we should find such an idea foreign to us, he suggests that may be due to the sad fact that we as a society have gradually lost our connection with the natural world. "As a consequence," he says, "our world is now imperiled by our lack of sensitivity to the whole. If we wish to preserve our world, we must first find our Mind by recovering our connections with the heavens and the Earth . . . to begin once more to talk with St. Francis to the creatures."

Whether you believe that you can communicate with your dog through mental telepathy or whether you feel only that you can develop a greater sensitivity to its unique sign language, the following exercises are designed to create a deeper rapport between you and your dog.

Psychics advise that if you truly wish to develop a mind linkup with your dog, first of all you must believe that it is possible to achieve such a melding of minds, that such a psychic phenomenon as telepathy truly exists. Once you admit to such a belief in mental communication, then you must be persuaded to accept the possibilities of your own capabilities. In order to achieve deep levels of mental rapport with your dog, first comes acknowledgment, then comes awareness.

When you first attempt to communicate with your dog, Penelope Smith advises you to keep things on a simple basis. "Which is not to say that dogs are simple beings," she stressed. "Many of them have been around the block a few times and have many tales to tell. But it is important for people to communicate clearly their thoughts, intentions, and mental images so their dogs do not get confused."

Here is an exercise that practicing psychics say will enable you to make telepathic transfer with your dog. Remember that it is important that you believe that such communication is possible and that you attempt to repeat the exercise at about the same time each day until satisfactory results are achieved.

Sit quietly for a few moments in a place away from the immediate physical presence of your dog. Stay still until you have quieted all of your senses.

Visualize the vastness of space, of infinity, or eternity. Understand that within such an array of possible universes there are an endless number of possible connections between all living brains. In the meaninglessness of our attempts to mark time in eternity, all exists as an eternal now.

See yourself sitting in a golden circle that is beginning to grow. Visualize the golden circle growing until it occupies the entire area of the room or place where you are sitting.

Know and understand that this golden circle that surrounds you has the ability to touch all the forces of nature around you.

Know and understand that this golden circle has the power to blend with the Intelligence that fills all of space.

Know and understand that this golden circle has the power to allow your consciousness to meld into oneness with All-That-Is.

Now clearly visualize your dog. See it plainly. Feel its presence.

In your mind, speak to your dog as if it were sitting there before you. Do not speak aloud. Speak to your dog mentally.

Breathe in three comfortably deep breaths. This will give you added power to energize the broadcasting station that exists in your psyche.

Mentally relay — then repeat twice — the message that you wish your dog to receive from you. On the simplest level, this could be a command, such as "Bring me the ball!" or "Fetch the stick!"

Give your dog a minute or so to respond. If there appears to be no immediate response, repeat the mental message two more times — or until your pet responds. However, you should never keep at this exercise until you grow weary of it or bored. You must always maintain a fresh, enthusiastic attitude in order to achieve the best and most successful results.

On a deeper level, this technique may be used to correct any of your dog's bad habits. In this case, the command might be, "Don't chew my shoes!" or "Don't have any more accidents in the house!"

By the same token, the exercise may also be utilized to intensify your dog's good habits. "Good dog, not to make a mess with your bowl. Good dog!" or "Good dog, always be nice to the neighbor children. Good dog!"

After continued practice, psychics say, the results you achieve will be quite dramatic, and you will have progressed much farther along the rewarding path of having established a firm telepathic line of communication with your dog.

CHAPTER 12
THE MENACE OF DOGNAPPING

PIKA WAS DOGNAPPED RIGHT IN FRONT OF HIS HUMAN COMPANION

Our friend and colleague Paul Dale Roberts said that his Pika looks like the dog seen in the once popular TV show *Frasier.*

"Everyone wanted him," Paul said. "So much so that on one day he was actually kidnapped — or should I say dognapped?

"I was walking T-Rex [his black chow] and Pika down a green belt [a designated natural walking path in urban areas] in Elk Grove, California. Pika is a ball of energy and loves to run ahead of me and T-Rex. So on this day, he was twenty feet ahead of us and a van pulls over. A woman comes out of the van and snatches Pika up and throws him into her van and drives off.

"I yell at her, 'Hey, that's my dog!' I started running after her, without any success. For seven days, I scoured the neighborhood looking for Pika and that van, again

315

without any success.

"On the eighth day, I hear a strange knocking on my door. I open the door and it's Pika! Somehow he escaped the lady dognapper and made it back home safely. He was so happy to be back home and wouldn't stop licking me! I could only wonder how he escaped.

"Pika is still with me. He is now thirteen years old and his companion is Hi-Pee, a brown corkie [a Yorkie–cocker spaniel hybrid]. Hi-Pee has his own unique personality. When I leave for work, he will position himself on the couch and look out the window, waiting for me to come home. There is something about man's best friend — they truly harbor the essence of unconditional love."

Two Million Dogs Are Dognapped Each Year

Although the average dognapper may not have the gall and recklessness to grab a dog off the street in full view of the startled owner, the nonprofit organization Last Chance for Animals based in Los Angeles estimates that two million dogs are stolen annually. Pet Lynx, a companion animal registry, has statistics indicating that one million dogs go missing in Canada every year.

As frightening and distasteful as it seems to dog lovers, some gentle pets are stolen to be sold to those who run illegal dogfights. The horror of so mistreating an animal bred to be a companion to children that he could be transformed into a killer dog, fighting for the entertainment of men more primitive than the dogs who entertain them with savage attacks on their fellow creatures, is the stuff of nightmares.

Other dogs are stolen with the goal of selling them to puppy mills for breeding purposes.

Incredibly, some dogs are stolen for ransom. In her article "Dognapped! Frightening Facts of Pet Theft" (*Modern Dog Magazine*), Yvonne Brooks disclosed that a family from Glendale, Colorado, paid $1,500 to get their Yorkshire terrier back after he was taken from their car.

Brooks quoted Linda Field, a former CBS journalist who now runs Findfido.com from her home in northern Pennsylvania, who told her that there are actually people who canvass neighborhoods looking for dogs to steal. Sadly, these professional dognappers steal dogs for various reasons, perhaps the most heinous one being to sell them to laboratories.

Stories of dognappers called "bunchers," thieves specializing in snatching dogs for sale to laboratories, had circulated for years, but many considered them rumors. Recently, Last Chance for Animals (www .lcanimal.org), a national, nonprofit organization dedicated to eliminating animal exploitation, proved that the despicable gangs did exist.

Atlanta resident Dorothy Pizzuti, director of the pet locator Web site dogdetective .com, told Brooks that her site averages 250,000 visitors every month. Pizzuti added the shocking statistic that in her experience about 10 percent of dogs reported as lost are actually victims of dognappers.

A certain number of dognappers steal people's dogs and sell them to other families. Pedigreed dogs, especially, can have very high price tags, often running into the thousands of dollars. Some dog lovers deficient in morality will buy a purebred potential dogshow prizewinner for easily half the price that a reputable dog breeder would charge them. True dog lovers should refuse to buy cut-price dogs with sloppy paperwork and inadequate background checks and force the resale of stolen dogs to dry up.

Owners Doubt Archie Could Travel 375 Miles in Two Days; A Dognapper Had to Have Grabbed Him

When Archie, a year-and-a-half-year-old West Highland terrier, disappeared just after Phil and Jackie Carr's other dog, a two-and-a-half-year-old cockapoo named Elle, had a litter of eight puppies, Phil commented wryly that maybe Archie was a "deadbeat dad" and had split.

All kidding aside, both of the Carrs took the disappearance of Archie very seriously.

On Monday, March 3, 2008, when they noticed that Archie was missing, they assumed that he had managed to sneak out the door — a misdeed that he had committed on previous occasions — and stepped out to enjoy the neighborhood near their Redding, California, home.

On Archie's previous unauthorized neighborhood excursions, he had just hung around, checked out the immediate area, and came home when he was called.

After a more than reasonable period of time calling and searching for their terrier, the Carrs sensed that this time was different. Their beloved Archie was missing.

The next day, they checked all the local pounds and shelters and were told that there was no such dog currently in their log-books or cages.

Now they were really worried, and they tacked up missing dog flyers wherever permissible. If anyone spotted Archie, they would see that he wore a collar with his name on it and the Carrs' telephone number. He also carried a microchip in his shoulder that bore his full name — Archibald McDonald.

On Thursday, the Carrs received a telephone call from the Valley Oaks Animal Shelter 375 miles from their home in Redding. According to a representative of the shelter, Archie had appeared bedraggled and collarless at 3:00 P.M., scratching at the door of a woman's home in Visalia. In spite of his being collarless, she let him sleep in her laundry room before she drove him to Valley Oaks the next day.

In Phil Carr's opinion, someone driving around their neighborhood in Redding snatched Archie when he disobeyed house orders and sneaked out of the door on Monday night. Carr found it difficult to accept that his fifteen-pound West Highland terrier could have covered 375 miles from Redding to Visalia in two days. Although his Westie is hardy and energetic, Carr believed that Archie had some unwanted assistance in his journey.

Jackie Carr told Dylan Darling of the *Redding News* (March 15, 2008) that she also was convinced that someone stole Archie, but she said that she will be mindful of the varying degrees of doggy trauma that Archibald may have felt when a batch of eight puppies suddenly arrived at the Carr household. She wanted to make him feel loved and very important to them, so he will not sneak out of the house again.

CELEBRITIES' DOGS ARE SPECIAL PREY FOR DOGNAPPERS

As one might suppose, dogs owned by celebrities are not immune to dognappers and might very well be more vulnerable because of the allure that a ransom might be gotten for the return of the pet.

Paris Hilton's Tinkerbell

At one time, hotel heiress Paris Hilton owned seventeen dogs, mostly Chihuahuas, and housed them in a special canine mansion, a scaled-down replica of her own. The ornate doghouse was situated in her backyard and contained furniture and a chandelier that were also precise replicas of the ones in her own luxurious home in Los Angeles.

On August 11, 2004, her special favorite, Tinkerbell, was found to be missing from the pampered pack, and Paris was both panicked and distraught, proclaiming that the Chihuahua was like a child to her. In the likelihood that Tinkerbell had been dognapped for ransom — a very likely possibility — Wendy White, the Hilton family personal assistant, claimed that the missing dog was really her Napoleon, and posters were placed all over Los Angeles, offering up to a $5,000 reward.

Although few details about how Tinkerbell was returned to Paris were ever made public, the fortunate Chihuahua did come home to a favored place in the doggy mansion.

Vanessa Williams's Enzo

On Memorial Day 2007, singer-actress Vanessa Williams spotted what she considered a suspicious van driving by her home in suburban New York. Later in the day, when she checked on her Yorkshire terrier, Enzo, who had been in the fenced-in yard, she was horrified to find him missing. Police who investigated her report did not wish to fuel rumors of a celebrity dognapper in the area. They suggested at best that Enzo might be wandering the neighborhood or at worst had been lured away by hungry coyotes.

Fortunately, reports DogChannel.com, Williams had had Enzo implanted with a microchip, and after a few stressful days filled with worry for the dog so loved by herself and her four children, a veterinarian in Connecticut scanned a lost terrier and found the microchip ID. In October 2007, Vanessa Williams became an active supporter of the Animal Haven Shelter in Soho and helped to launch their Bring Pets Home microchipping initiative.

CRUEL DOGNAPPERS TAKE EIGHTY-SIX-YEAR-OLD WIDOWER'S BUDDY; DOG RESCUE SQUAD REUNITES THEM AFTER FIVE YEARS

Eighty-two-year-old Walter Smith bought Buddy, a yellow Labrador puppy, shortly after the death of his wife, Jane. Buddy was a perfect companion for the widower. He was loving, gentle, and always good-natured.

In 1998, after a few months of very close bonding with the Lab, Smith decided to move from his home in Illinois to Titusville, Florida. The young Lab adapted well to the move, and for the next four years, Walter and Buddy were constant companions.

One day when Smith was shopping in the

Home Depot in Merritt Island, he left Buddy in the van with a couple of the windows lowered several inches so the dog wouldn't become overheated while he was in the store. When Smith came out of Home Depot, his beloved companion Buddy had vanished from the front seat of the van. Buddy had been dognapped.

Buddy, Walter Smith often remarked after the Lab's disappearance, was just too friendly. If any stranger approached him while he was in the van, Buddy wouldn't growl or bark, he would just start wiggling his body and wagging his tail in the friendliest of ways. Walter was certain that someone who had sized up the yellow Lab as a great pet for themselves or their kids just reached in the window of the van, opened the door, and led Buddy away.

In retrospect, Smith believes that it was Buddy's good nature that brought about many years of sorrow and suffering, both for the man and the dog.

Walter Smith began the frustrating and demanding ritual that must be endured by all those who love their missing dogs and truly wish to be reunited with them. He called all the local animal shelters and veterinarians; he ran ads in the newspaper and neighborhood shopping guides; he plastered posters wherever people of good-will would allow him to do so.

Soon he began receiving calls from people who told him that they had sighted a yellow Lab in such and such a neighborhood and insisted that they should receive the reward that Smith had offered. Again and again, Walter patiently attempted to explain that the reward would come upon deliverance of Buddy, not an ambiguous sighting. Especially painful were the telephone calls that told him that the individual had allegedly witnessed a yellow Lab being struck and killed by a truck or a car.

Weeks passed into months without any word of Buddy. Walter could only accept the sad reality that whoever had taken him wasn't about to return him. Walter prayed that whoever had dognapped Buddy was treating him kindly and decently. The gentle yellow Lab surely did not deserve a life of mistreatment and abuse. Just thinking of anyone mistreating Buddy would cause Walter to begin to cry.

After several months had gone by, a police officer who had handled Smith's missing dog report and who had a great deal of sympathy for the elderly man brought Walter a little papillon puppy that the animal shelter had found wandering in the streets.

The puppy had no collar, no ID of any kind, and was obviously homeless. The officer said that in spite of a rough beginning, the little dog seemed responsive to kindness and appeared willing to extend his own canine love.

Walter welcomed the dog that he named Pappy into his life, but he still thought often about Buddy and still retained the hope that one day the yellow Lab would come back into his life.

Walter Smith maintained that hope for five long years. And then one day in November 2007, he received a telephone call from a woman who claimed that she had found Buddy.

The woman was Beth Beeco, who, with her sister, Linda Rodman, live in Edgewater and conduct a kind of two-woman dog rescue squad. They had spotted a yellow Lab loose in the street in Edgewater, and they checked around, attempting to find who the owner was.

After drawing blanks for immediate identification, Beth went online to a lost dog Web site and saw a photo of Buddy, decked out in his red collar. When they managed to approach Buddy on the street and examine him closely, they found Walter Smith's name and telephone number on one of the Lab's dog tags.

Beeco and Rodman arranged to meet with Smith and bring him together with the dog that he had lost so long ago. They admitted to one another that they had mixed feelings about the reunion, because they and their other ten dogs had grown attached to Buddy within just a few days.

However, when they witnessed how happy Walter was to see Buddy again after five years, they consoled themselves with the thought that they had performed a beautiful and righteous act by bringing the two old companions together again. They knew that Buddy would have a wonderful life with his rightful owner.

In the meantime, Walter was very much enjoying his reunion with his old pal. Buddy curled up at Walter's feet, just as he had done so many years ago. Walter was bemused that Buddy fell asleep on the couch, just as he had done so often when they lived together after moving from Illinois.

Walter could see that Buddy was the same loving dog that he had always been, and he was nearly overcome with emotion when the full realization struck him that he had at last been reunited with a beloved dog that he thought he would never see again.

As Walter sat alone with his thoughts, he

began to reconsider the situation from a larger perspective. He was now ninety-one years old. Could he still handle a big dog like the yellow Lab, sleeping now so peacefully on the couch? Could he provide him with the exercise and walks that he would need to keep him physically well and fit?

Walter looked down at Pappy, lovingly curled up at his feet. Little Pappy hadn't been too happy to see his owner welcome that big old Lab into their home. And, from his doggy viewpoint, he could probably make quite an argument that he had served Walter well these past five years without the help of Buddy.

Buddy was now nine years old. Walter wondered what kind of life his old friend had had since he was stolen from the van. Had his new owner been kind or had he abused him and eventually turned him out into the streets where the two dear ladies found him?

The next morning, Walter, his voice faltering, called Linda Rodman and Beth Beeco and told them that he had decided that Buddy would be better served if he returned to their home.

The two sisters wept with joy. They agreed to keep Buddy and to love him and treat him well; and when they returned Buddy to their pack of loving dogs, they said that they, too, were thrilled to have Buddy back home with them.

Linda and Beth take Buddy to Walter Smith and Pappy's home in Titusville on regular visits. Buddy always goes directly to Walter to receive some cuddling, then jumps up on the couch, his favorite comfort place. Eventually, Pappy seemed to get over his jealousy and recognize that his and Walter's family had just grown considerably larger. Besides, Linda and Beth often brought him new chew toys.

Walter told a reporter from *Florida Today* in December 2007 that he still has dreams about Buddy and still thinks about him every day. He explained that he had bought Buddy right after his wife, Jane, had passed away and that the yellow Lab had been an important part of his life for five years.

Walter mused that he wished that he could take proper care of Buddy, but at the age of ninety-one, little Pappy was more his speed. Since Linda Rodman and Beth Beeco agreed to bring Buddy to Titusville whenever he wanted to see him, Walter Smith figured that such an arrangement was a most wonderful thing.

An Eleven-Year-Old Pomeranian Rescued from Dognappers Who Had Taken Him 568 Miles from Home

In early January 2002, according to the *Corpus Christi Caller Times* (February 9, 2002), Alonzo Gutierrez and his thirteen-year-old daughter, Megan, were returning home when Alonzo saw a sight that he considered one of the strangest that he had ever witnessed.

A large blue van appeared to be chasing a tiny Pomeranian down the street.

Alonzo and Megan stopped to watch the strange spectacle. Megan became upset at once over the huge vehicle that seemed to want to run the little Pomeranian down. The wee tan dog was running just as fast as its legs, no longer than pencils, would carry it.

Suddenly, before the eyes of the astounded Gutierrezes, a skinny little boy jumped out of the blue van and began to chase the Pomeranian on foot.

"Just what is going on?" Alonzo and his daughter wondered aloud. If the little dog belonged to the people in the van, they should be able to stop and call to the dog. The two of them became suspicious that things were not right, and they stopped to observe the action more closely.

The little boy could run very fast, but, amazingly, the Pomeranian could run faster. Alonzo would not claim to be an expert on dogs, but to his layman's eyes, the Pomeranian was certainly no pup. In fact, the little dog appeared to be quite old.

At last the boy gave up, jumped back into the blue van, and the vehicle roared away, obviously giving up the chase.

This puzzled Alonzo and Megan even more. If the Pomeranian were indeed their dog, why leave him alone in a strange city? If Alonzo had seen correctly, the blue van bore Oklahoma plates — and they were in Corpus Christi, Texas. Maybe they just didn't want the cute little fellow anymore?

Alonzo suggested that Megan try to catch the dog. At least they would bring it to an animal shelter where it would receive humane treatment. He could not in all conscience leave such a little dog to the mercy of the streets of Corpus Christi.

Capturing the dog did not prove difficult for Megan. In fact, once the Pomeranian saw that Megan was chasing after it, it turned around, ran toward her, and jumped into her arms. The little dog was puffing heavily and was obviously nearly completely exhausted. It had obviously recognized a friendly face and a comforting pair of arms.

When they reached home, Judy Gutierrez cleaned the Pomeranian's collar and discovered that the brave fellow was suitably named King. They were quite surprised to learn that King belonged to the Dye family of Crescent, Oklahoma. Megan did a quick check in the atlas and noted that King was 568 miles from home.

It was clear to the Gutierrez family that King had been dognapped by the family in the blue van. Fortunately, the thieves hadn't been bright enough to remove his collar.

Judy Gutierrez noticed that one of the digits of the Dyes' telephone number had been gouged away, so she had to dial the ten possible combinations before she reached Shirley Dye in Crescent City.

Shirley and J. L. Dye were emotionally overwhelmed with the wonderful news that the Gutierrez family had reclaimed their dog from the thieves. Eleven-year-old King had been a cherished member of the Dye household since he was a puppy. He had disappeared from their daughter's yard in Oklahoma City while they had been on vacation in 2001. Although their daughter had felt terrible and had at first blamed herself for King's becoming lost, the Dyes found a trail of jerky treats that the dognappers had used to lure King out of the yard.

After months of following the regular regimen of posting notices, placing ads in local newspapers, calling lost-pet hotlines, and regularly offering prayers for his return, the Dyes had given up all hope of ever seeing their beloved King again.

In two days, Shirley and J. L. Dye arrived at the Gutierrez home, fully equipped with camcorders and cameras to record the return of the mighty King, who had never stopped fighting his abductors and trying his best to escape their clutches. Judy Gutierrez said later that everyone was crying enough tears to nearly drown the courageous King.

Although he had suffered abuse and had been forced to endure stresses placed on his powers of endurance, King had only lost four of his usual ten pounds during the ordeal. A veterinarian also recommended the removal of two teeth that may have become loosened as King continually attempted to chew the bonds that tied him to the dognappers.

THEIR PUG WAS DOGNAPPED TWICE BEFORE THEY GOT THE MESSAGE TO BE CAUTIOUS*

Most of us have learned the hard way that some actions once done cannot be undone and we must suffer the consequences. When Amber tied Porter, her two-year-old pug, to the bicycle stand in front of the neighborhood market that December afternoon in 2005, she thought no harm could come to him if she quickly ran inside to pick up a box of cereal and a quart of milk. However, even though she was only gone for five minutes or so, when she came out of the market, Porter was missing.

Amber said that she had tied him securely by his leather leash and told him to stand still and not to pull on it. She called his name and walked around the neighborhood, hoping that he had just managed to pull the leash loose from the stand and do a little unauthorized exploring in the immediate area. She kept hoping that was the case. She prayed that no one had actually taken her sweet little Porter.

Although a pug looks something like a cross between a bulldog and a Pekingese

* Amber and Vince only wish their first names to be used in this entry.

and may give the impressive of being a pretty tough little guy, Amber soon learned that Porter was very sensitive and could even be rather timid. He might appear as though he were a big dog in a fourteen-pound body, but he was more friendly to strangers than aggressive.

All the way home to their apartment, Amber kept hearing the words that she knew Vince, her husband, would say to her:

1. She was always too trusting of other people. Who would tie a dog to a bicycle stand in a place like the Bronx and expect the dog to be there when she left the market?
2. Taking Porter for a walk meant that and only that. If she had to do some shopping, bring the dog home first.
3. Hadn't he been opposed to getting a dog in the first place? They had only a small apartment. One day, when they got a bigger place or a house in the suburbs, they would get a dog.

Amber later remarked that five minutes after she had entered their apartment without Porter in tow, Vince had covered all those major points, though not necessarily in that order.

She knew that Porter meant so much more to Vince than he would ever admit. Every night when he got home, he would play with the pug, and he would often surprise Porter by bringing him a new chew toy. On many evenings, Porter would fall asleep across "Daddy's" lap while Vince was watching the news before bedtime.

The next day Vince left work early to put up posters all over the neighborhood. Although they hardly had any money to spare, Vince offered a hundred-dollar reward. When Amber appeared somewhat surprised, Vince just shrugged and said that he wished it could be a thousand dollars and a guarantee that they would get Porter back safely. Amber used her lunch hour to call all the veterinarians and animal shelters in the area.

That night at dinner, Vince expressed his concern about the weather turning colder. Although it had been a mild autumn, it was now edging into November, and he was worried about Porter somewhere out there on the streets, trying to keep warm.

Later that same evening, just as they were preparing for bed, Amber and Vince heard a scratching at their apartment door. They were joyful beyond words when they beheld

Porter, but their cries of happiness soon turned to expressions of concern. The little pug was bleeding around both ears, and the leather collar around his neck had been replaced by a coarse noose of twine. Porter had obviously been stolen and held by someone who had treated him cruelly and bound him with twine. The determined pug had chewed away at his restraints until he freed himself and made it home to his owners' apartment.

The next day, Vince called his office and said that he would be in late. He took Porter to a veterinarian, who said that the tough little pooch had taken some hard whacks, but he was basically in good shape.

Unfortunately, Amber said, Porter's misadventures were not yet over. This time it was Vince who bore the mantle of guilt.

He had been walking Porter when he ran into a couple of friends from his old neighborhood. While he was standing on a corner talking to the guys, a local high school opened its doors to unleash a crowd of teenagers into the streets. A couple of girls stopped and asked to pet Porter. Vince assured them that he wouldn't bite, then went back to catching up on old times.

When Vince came back to the present, two weeks before Christmas in 2005, he saw that

Porter's leash had been neatly cut and their beloved pug was once again missing. Sometime while he was talking with his old buddies and dodging teenagers rushing out of the high school, someone had dognapped Porter for a second time.

Amber said that Vince was totally devastated when he returned to the apartment. He berated himself for hours about his being so careless with their precious Porter. She knew that he would sit up all night in his recliner, tormenting himself for having been so irresponsible.

The next morning was Saturday, and around eleven o'clock there came a knock at their apartment door. Amber opened it to see two teenage boys standing there. One of them was holding Porter, who squirmed out of the boy's arms and ran into the apartment to jump on Vince, who was still sitting in his recliner.

According to the boys, they had seen a classmate cut Porter free and run off with him while Vince was talking with his friends on the street corner. Vince and his friends were so busy talking and the wave of high school students had pretty much engulfed the street, so the dognapper had made an easy snatch.

About three blocks away, Porter, who had

been struggling to get free, managed to bite the boy and run away when the young thug dropped him. The two boys who were in pursuit of the thief finally cornered Porter in an alley and took him home with them.

The boys explained that they didn't know Vince or his friends or how to get in contact with him to return Porter. Then one boy's sister brought out one of Vince's old reward posters with the picture of Porter on it. She had saved it because she had said that one day she wanted to get a little dog that looked just like that one.

Vince and Amber thanked the boys and told them how much their kindness in returning Porter meant to them.

Vince, who was always so smooth with his words in his sales job, now stammered awkwardly when he explained that he really didn't have the hundred dollars that the reward poster promised. He could give them twenty dollars, though, and he hoped they would consider that adequate recompense for their trouble.

The boys looked at each other in astonishment. They didn't want any reward. They just wanted to see that the cute little dog was returned to his rightful owners. They wished Amber and Vince a Merry Christmas, said good-bye to Porter, and walked down the hallway.

Vince had tears in his eyes when he put one arm around Amber, held Porter to his chest with the other, and shouted a resounding "Merry Christmas" after the boys.

It will not surprise anyone that Vince and Amber's New Year's resolution was to be much more vigilant when walking their beloved pug, Porter, on the city streets.

HERCULES DISAPPEARED WHEN HIS HOME WAS BURGLARIZED, TEN MONTHS LATER — FOUND WITHOUT A MINUTE TO SPARE

As authors, we always maintain that truth is stranger than fiction, especially when it comes to bizarre coincidences. If a writer injects an "impossible coincidence" into a fiction story, such as someone arriving just in the nick of time to save her dog from being shipped off to an unknown fate, the reader will groan and say that life just doesn't happen that way. But sometimes it does, and in even stranger ways than any writer could imagine.

On February 14, 2001 — Valentine's Day, the day for love, to add insult to injury — the Sisco family of Clearwater, Florida, had their home burglarized and Hercules, their revered family dog, disappeared.

Although it could not be determined whether Hercules had been dognapped by the thieves or had become confused and run away in the excitement, the Siscos' three-year-old, seventy-pound tan with black and white markings American Staffordshire terrier mix had vanished. The Sisco family chose to believe that their courageous Hercules had chased after the burglar's vehicle until he had become lost and unable to find his way back home.

It is at this point that we must assume the omniscient point of view and inform the reader that after reports of a wandering dog in numerous neighborhoods in Clearwater, a large tan dog with black and white markings was picked up by animal control officers and taken to the local dog shelter. After the dog was given a bath and checked over by a veterinarian, he was put up for adoption. Because the big mutt was so personable, it was not long before a family chose him and took him home with them.

Months passed. The Sisco family considered acquiring another dog, but the hurt in their hearts from losing Hercules was still too strong. Lisa, the mother, raised the point that having a little puppy around the house would help them get over Hercules. Her husband and eight-year-old daughter stated firmly that they were not ready to "get over" Hercules. He was such a good friend, such a wonderful dog, so intelligent — and don't forget how brave he was to chase after those burglars. Why, he may even have given his life attempting to protect their property. No animal other than a dog will die protecting its owner's property.

The argument to get another dog in the Sisco family was tabled for the time being.

Meanwhile, as a few more months passed, that big, tan dog with black and white markings that was so readily adopted from the animal shelter had most definitely decided that he did not like his new home. The family was shocked by his behavior, because he seemed so amiable and pleasant in the cage at the animal shelter. However, he had caused them no end of mayhem and commotion, and they were going to have their Christmas ruined by the antics of an unruly dog. So it was straight to the local Humane Society with him that he may find peace with another unsuspecting family.

It was now December 18, several months after the Sisco family's decision not to attempt to replace Hercules in their hearts quite so soon. Lisa Sisco had decided that her vote overrided that of her husband's and her daughter's, and she used her lunch hour to visit the Humane Society of North Pinellas in Clearwater.

Just as Lisa was about to approach the kennel in which Hercules has been placed, a society employee told a volunteer that the big, tan dog with the black and white markings was supposed to have been given a bath long ago. The volunteer nodded his head, acknowledged the task, and promised to give the big mutt a good soaking and make him spic-and-span clean right after he finished his lunch.

That was close. If there hadn't been that delay, Hercules would not have been in the kennel area when Lisa entered.

Lisa took one look at the big tan dog with the black and white markings and shouted, "Hercules!"

Members of the Humane Society of North Pinellas who witnessed the reunion said that the big dog almost broke through the cage to be at Lisa's side.

Rick Chaboudy, executive director of the Humane Society of North Pinellas, was quoted as saying that if Hercules had been bathed fifteen minutes before Lisa Sisco entered the kennel area, he would not have been there for her to see him. "Things like this don't happen very often," Mr. Chaboudy said to Katherine Gazella of the

the *St. Petersburg Times* (December 19, 2001), "but when they do, especially at Christmastime, they do make you think of miracles." And of coincidences that are stranger than fiction.

CHAPTER 13
COMMON REASONS
DOGS GO MISSING

It is a sad situation when owners abandon their dogs because they have decided after the fact of acquiring them that they did so under the wrong "circumstances." It is even sadder when responsible and caring owners discover that their beloved dogs are missing.

How do loving dog owners react when they return home from work or picking up the kids and find the backyard gate unlatched — and their dog nowhere in sight?

Here are some typical responses:

- They spend desperate hours searching, calling its name, asking friends and neighbors to help them find their beloved canine family member.
- They are puzzled: Why did their dog leave the yard? Why would he or she want to venture out of the confines of home territory?

- They are fearful: Did someone take their dog? Someone who would mistreat it; someone who would not know its favorite snack; someone who wouldn't care for its comfort; someone who wouldn't give it that little scratch behind the ear that it loves so much.
- After a few hours of searching, they may even become a bit angry: He knows better than to run off like that. She should have stayed right in the backyard under the shade of the big oak tree.
- After several hours of looking everywhere that they think their dog might possibly be, they feel hurt: They really believed that the two of them had bonded. They really felt that he loved them. She certainly seemed to love those special treats that they gave her. Were they somehow mistreating the dog without being aware of their abuse? Were they simply unaware that their personalities never really meshed?

THE MOST COMMON REASONS WHY DOGS GO MISSING

Dr. Nicholas Dodman, founder of the Animal Behavior Clinic at Tufts University, lists seven reasons in his article "Dogs That

Run Away" (PetPlace.com) why some dogs who are loved and pampered are still inclined to wander away from home.

Reproductive drive. If the dog is not neutered, the odor of estrogen on the wind can travel great distances and the call to reproduce can drive out all human requests to be a good dog and stay in the yard. Dr. Dodman states that as with humans, the sexual urges are generated in the brain, not in the loins, and can cause either male or female dogs to develop compelling urges to break free of the boundaries imposed by their owners. As one of the world's most respected animal behaviorists, Dr. Dodman advises those responsible dog owners who have neutered their pets that castration does not reduce the roaming instinct for 10 percent of dogs. Still, he strongly recommends neutering as the best way to reduce the risk of roaming in an intact dog.

Boredom. Busy people who rush off to work leaving their dogs alone in the backyard or tied up all day, then return in late afternoon and early evening to unwind in the house and eat dinner before paying any attention to their canine companion may inadvertently drive their neglected pet to seek escape from a boring existence.

Predatory drive. Even though the dog may

be well fed, Dr. Dodman explains, "seeking and finding prey is one of the most powerful natural tendencies that dogs possess." Compelled by the atavistic urge of the hunt, the stalking and killing of worthy prey can provide a thrill like no other for the dog cooped up in a small yard.

Social reasons. Some dogs may retain the genetic memory of a time when they, like their wolf ancestors, maintained the den as home and considered another part of the forest as a kind of secondary residence in which to hang out for a time. Dr. Dodman cites examples of dogs that might wake up with their owners, see them off to work, then get out of the yard to wander over to one of the neighbors for breakfast, another for lunch, then be back at home to greet their owners' return.

Physical rewards. Food is a powerful incentive to wander away from the yard for the dog who is not getting enough nourishment at home, or even if he feels that he is not being fed enough to satisfy him. Enticing smells from the neighbors' yard may lure a dog to wander first next door, then, perhaps, to explore farther away in the hope of finding additional goodies.

Thunderstorm phobia. Many owners have witnessed the fear exhibited by their dogs at the loud rumble and crashes of a thunderstorm. The frightened dog who is able to escape the yard or other confinement will run until he is confident that the booming storm noises have stopped. And by that time, he might be miles away from home in unfamiliar territory. Dr. Dodman comments that thunderstorm-phobic dogs sometimes become quite skilled at breaking out of the yard, jumping from windows, or leaping over high fences in a single bound as if they had super powers.

Abuse. The final reason that Dr. Dodman discusses is one that is much more uncommon: Though many people consider their dog to be a member of the family, there are still some cases when a dog is mistreated or abused in some way and that causes it to run away from its owner.

Along with Dr. Dodson, who considers it unlikely that very many contemporary dog owners would physically abuse their pets, we doubt that any readers who would be interested in the subject matter in the pages of this book would be deliberately cruel to their dog and thereby drive their canine to seek escape from inhumane treatment. However, we will caution that because of busy personal schedules, the owners of a wandering dog may have paid inadequate attention to their pet, thereby inflicting the mental cruelty of neglect and indifference. A dog who has become little more than an lawn ornament in the eyes of its owner may wish to dig its way out of the yard to explore its opportunities for love and attention elsewhere.

Echoing Dr. Dodson's warnings about dogs becoming bored in a backyard and being tempted to escape the dull confines, many experts remind dog owners to examine the boundary of their property, as well as the reliability of the gates and the sturdiness of the fence. Conscientious owners should also be aware of areas in the fence where their dog might easily dig its way under, enabling it to run free.

Another valuable tip to prevent your dog from going missing is to always keep it on a leash. The cautious dog owner will never let his/her dog off its leash while taking it for a walk around the block or while stopping for a potty break at a highway rest stop when going for a drive. The *Journal of American Veterinary Medical Association* (1995; 45) conducted studies that showed that 84 percent of dogs will take off on a run when they are let off a leash. And one certainly should not let one's dog off its leash when arriving at a vacation cabin in the woods.

If your dog is ultra-friendly and gregarious, it may come up to any stranger who pays attention to it. This is another reason to keep it on a leash when visiting a park or playground. If your dog wanders away from you, it may allow itself to be easily "adopted" by individuals looking for a pet to take home for the kids — or to sell.

If your dog is normally aloof and wary of strangers, does it warm to individuals who offer it treats? By permitting your dog to wander unattended in a public place for even a few moments, you may place it in danger from a dognapper with some tempting, tasty treats.

If your dog has phobias or fears, its anxiety may cause it to break away from you even if you do have it on a leash. A frightened dog can run heedlessly for miles before it stops. Later, when it finally stops running, even if responsible dog lovers may eventually manage to corral it and read the tags on its collar, they may not call you. The dog's trembling and fearfulness may cause them to assume that the dog is abused, leading them to either adopt your dog for themselves or deliver it to an animal shelter.

Be aware of how your dog responds to

other dogs when you have it on a leash. Does it become aggressive, passive, or frightened when it comes into close contact with another canine? Whatever your pet's response, be very alert and tighten your hold on the leash if the two or three dogs begin either a communal lovefest or an angry encounter. Far too many owners have had their dog go missing when it jerked the leash from their hands and ran off with another dog freed from its leash, or it ran off in fear after receiving a snarl and a warning nip from a canine stranger. Others report having their dog go missing when it tugged the leash out of their hand when it wanted to visit a dog walking with its owner on the other side of the street.

Dog expert Joe Wilkes also recommends having your dog's leash attached to a good collar that fits well around its neck. A substantial, well-fitting collar will prevent your dog from slipping out of it and getting loose, and it should carry your contact information in the form of your dog's identification tags in the event that it somehow runs free. Wilkes also cautions against having a fancy, decorative collar, rather than one that is functional.

Another useful tip advises dog owners not to decide to save a few dollars and leave their pet with friends or relatives when they go out of town or on vacation. Even if your parents or best friends may be generally familiar with your dog, it is unlikely that they know all its idiosyncrasies and peculiar preferences. In addition, it is also unlikely that your dog understands the concept of "vacation" or "weekend getaway" and may decide your leaving it with other humans is unacceptable, causing it to dig under a fence or dart out of an open door and head for home. All these things considered, many experts recommend that you select a trustworthy kennel to be your dog's residence during your absence.

And speaking of vacations, if you should decide to take your pet with you, many of the most popular getaway spots are prime areas for dognappers to work their nefarious trade. Another point to emphasize is that many of the most popular vacation spots and tourist attractions are prime areas in which dogs might get away and become lost.

It is certainly a good thing for lost dogs that there are individuals who are motivated to rescue dogs who have strayed from their homes or who have been separated from their owners due to a troubling list of possibilities. As we noted in the introduction, as many as four million dogs are lost or misplaced every year.

CELEBRITIES WHO RESCUE LOST DOGS

As we have noted a number of times in this book, several celebrities have taken up the issues of dog and animal rescue as their special causes. Here are two well-known personalities who have devoted many years to rescuing and adopting lost dogs.

Lisa Edelstein

Actress Lisa Edelstein, who played Dr. Cuddy for seven years on the television series *House,* has been rescuing lost animals since she was a girl of eleven in suburban Wayne, New Jersey. After attending New York University's Tisch School of the Arts in the 1980s, she relocated to Los Angeles, where she and her roommate took in a four-month-old stray shepherd mix that had been struck by a car. Lisa took the female pup to a veterinarian, then adopted her and named her Sandwich. Lisa and her roommate went their separate ways, but Lisa and Sandwich were together until Sandwich died at age thirteen.

Lisa continued to adopt stray dogs as her career progressed. Wolf E., an Alaskan husky mix, was found wandering on a film set by a friend, but the dog, suffering from poor vision, seizures, and difficulty walking, become attached to the actress, so she took him home to live with her and Sandwich — and a couple of other strays that she had adopted.

She found Bumpa, a mutt, near Dodger Stadium in the 1990s, just as her career was really taking off with regular appearances on *Ally McBeal*, *The West Wing*, and *The Practice*. That was when she met Cesar Millan, who gave her some advice on how best to integrate Bumpa with her already existing pack of dogs. She had heard about Cesar by word of mouth from pet store owners as someone who had a way with dogs. That was long before he became *the* Cesar, widely known and famous on television as the Dog Whisperer.

Lisa takes time from her busy career to volunteer with the Best Friends Animal Society and help people with the adoption of dogs. She cautions that many people who want to rescue strays mean well, but they may later find out that caring for a pet is too big a responsibility for them. The danger, then, is that they may once again turn their adopted pet into a stray. One has to be prepared to do the work of caring properly for a dog, she advises.

Currently, Shazam and Kapow are "major joys" in her life, Lisa Edelstein told Larry Sutton for the August 29, 2011, issue of *Cesar's Way*. Lisa said that one has to take time to communicate with one's dogs, no matter how one might be feeling. "And more important," she added, "a little bit of love goes a long way with them. It takes very little to make the dogs feel happy. And then you feel better about yourself."

John O'Hurley

John O'Hurley, who achieved fame with his recurring role as J. Peterman on the television series *Seinfeld,* is another celebrity who is a dog lover and, on occasion, a dog rescuer. Thanksgiving Day 2011 marked the tenth year that O'Hurley has hosted NBC's broadcast of the Purina National Dog Show with dog show expert David Frei. In his book *Before Your Dog Can Eat Your Homework, First You Have to Do It* (2007), O'Hurley shares many lessons that he has learned from dogs over the years, beginning with his childhood dog, Taffy.

In 1994, when O'Hurley moved from New York to Los Angeles, Scoshi, a Maltese, who is now twenty-one, was his companion on the long drive. Not long after they arrived, the two fast friends found Betty, an unusual Labrador/dachshund mix, wandering in the hills near their home. Betty was terribly scrawny and nearly starved, but once O'Hurley had nursed her back to health, she proved to be one of the gentlest dogs that he had ever known.

O'Hurley has a television program in development that has as its theme the importance of fitting the right dog with the right owner. "I feel that a lot of dogs are abandoned because it was the wrong fit in the first place," he told *Celebrity Dogs* (August 29, 2011). "We need to match the dog to the circumstances."

LEARNING TO SPEAK DOG

Years ago, we determined that we could better comprehend our dogs' mental processes if we just took a few moments to observe their body language. We highly recommend that all dog owners take the time to learn to speak Dog. We cannot claim that we are able to distinguish with unfailing accuracy which aspects of our dogs' body stances and movements were distinctly their own and which were universal messages in the doggy dictionary of sign language, but we have been able to use all of the following signs to "talk" to many dogs over the past five decades.

When your dog lifts a forepaw toward you, it appears to be akin to saying, "I would like . . ." or asking "May I have . . . ?"

Sometimes the gesture seems to mean, "Please pay attention to me." But in all instances, the movement appears to sign a request of some sort.

If your dog's ears are pulled back, and it looks at you with soulful eyes, it is relaying its distress or unhappiness with a situation. It may be something as serious as displeasure with some present condition that you have imposed on your pet, or it may be a matter as simple to remedy as giving your dog some more love. Perhaps you have been a bit too busy with other concerns to pay adequate attention to your dog's emotional needs.

There are numerous erudite theories as to why your dog licks your hand, but unless you've spilled gravy on your fingers, a soft lick on your hand from your dog always translates to us as "I love you."

When your dog rolls over on its back and exposes its stomach, it is apologizing for having done something that it knows upset or angered you. Perhaps it has made a mess, and you have raised your voice in anger or displeasure.

On the other hand, when your dog's ears

are pricked up and its lips are raised around its teeth, it is telling you for whatever reason to back off: "Don't mess with me just now, please. I am upset about something. But don't worry. You know me. My irritation will pass very quickly."

On those occasions when your dog holds its tail high, wags it vigorously, lowers its torso onto its forepaws, sticks its rear end up, and "smiles" with its mouth open, it is signaling you that it is in a playful mood. Perhaps it is time for a walk or to toss the Frisbee. When Moses, our black Labrador, would go into this stance — and we would agree that it was time for a walk or a drive — he would usually follow this posture with a joyful jump in the air, indicating his extreme pleasure.

Just because your dog is wagging its tail, it is not necessarily telling you that it is happy. A rapid movement of the tail can also mean that your dog is excited about something and might even be uncertain how to proceed. A few words of assurance and love would be well advised at this point.

And now, while you are learning to speak Dog, a few words about respecting your Dog's senses — for your mutual benefit:

Be considerate in your understanding that

your dog's sense of smell is its most power-ful faculty. Be careful not to spray noxious odors or powerful disinfectants near your dog.

Also remember that your dog first identi-fies even you by your unique smell.

It is because dogs rely so greatly on their sense of smell that not long ago the media carried an account of an apartment dweller who was attacked by his own dog when he came through the door wearing a different brand of cologne, sunglasses, and a coat that he had borrowed from a friend.

Although there are those who claim their dogs love to guzzle beer, many canines take an instant disliking to anyone with alcohol on their breath. The same can be said of tobacco smoke. Many dogs will act in an aggressive manner around cigarette, cigar, or pipe smokers.

While your dog's sense of hearing might be somewhat more sensitive than yours under certain conditions, it is easily con-fused or irritated by high-pitched frequen-cies, such as sirens, whistles, certain musi-cal instruments, and squealing children — especially if he or she is used to being quietly alone with Mommy and Daddy. Remember to be considerate in this regard and don't subject your dog's ears to music played at the threshold of pain when you are taking a road trip, either.

We are certain that you will learn to speak Dog by becoming more observant and attuned to your dog's efforts to communicate with you. We must say that we are becoming more proficient in Dog as we learn to "listen" to what our dog says.

Hans, our present companion, a Yorkshire–bichon frisé mix, was acquired at a very young age, and because our offices are in our home and we are full-time writers, he has always been with us 24/7. We have learned many new words in Dog, and we are delighted that so much constant companionship has encouraged Hans very often to attempt to speak our language, at least by mimicking some of our vocal sounds and speech patterns. With each dog with whom we have been privileged to share our lives, we have learned more about interspecies communication. Try it. It is wonderful fun and a great blessing.

We have also learned that the basic key to communication with our dogs has always been genuine respect and affection. We remain convinced that love is the greatest power in the universe and that it works as effectively with animals as with humans.

We have long believed that the intelligence

of a dog may be largely dependent upon the mental-spiritual linkup that occurs between the dog and its owner.

We are certain that we have all known dogs whom we suspected were innately more intelligent than their owners. And surely we suspect that it is largely impossible to rank all members of a particular breed as more intelligent than all other members of another breed as some canine experts have done.

We suggest that the intelligence displayed by your dog will be directly proportional to the time you spend with your dog and the level of bonding that you have permitted between you and your canine companion.

If you regard your dog as little more than an animated stuffed toy, then that is the level of intelligence that you are likely to receive from your pet.

If you consider your dog to be only a bit more than a utilitarian item in your home, something along the lines of an affectionate appliance, then you are likely to receive an appropriate utilitarian response from your dog.

But if you have found yourself a responsive dog (and, of course, there are degrees of sensitivity and responsiveness among canines, just as there are among humans), and if you are willing to commit to an attitude of openness, a full expression of respect, a wish to be caring, and a willingness to give and to receive unconditional love that will attempt to equal that which your dog holds for you, then you will witness a manifestation of communication with your dog beyond what you ever expected was possible. A beautiful, perhaps limitless mind link will occur that will allow you to gain a fuller understanding of the mysteries of God's continuing acts of creation.

CHAPTER 14
USEFUL TIPS TO HELP YOU FIND YOUR LOST DOG

IF YOUR DOG GOES MISSING . . .

If you should discover that your dog is missing, first take a few minutes to check with your neighbors. Do they have a dog or children with whom your dog likes to play on the occasional visit?

If you have older children in your home who have drivers' licenses, call their cell phones to be certain that they have not taken the family dog along for a drive.

Look around your immediate neighborhood. Is there a park or a path somewhere nearby where you take your dog on walks? If there are such doggy temptations near at hand, check them out as quickly as possible.

Once you are certain that your dog has gone missing, do not wait another minute to see if by chance he might suddenly return on his own. Do not rationalize that he or she might come home when it gets dark. If your dog has got out through an open gate, door, or window, you should assume the worst — that he was bored, lonely, or, if he/she has not been neutered, answered the call of sexual urges. Go immediately to nearby animal shelters to see if anyone has picked up your dog and dropped him off.

If your dog has not been found by a conscientious animal lover and brought to a shelter, return quickly to your home and begin to make posters to be put up in your area. Your signs need to be large, bright, and colorful. Be certain that the word "reward" is in large letters. If you live in a bilingual community, put up your signs written in both languages. An Internet search engine can provide you with a translation of your text.

It is very important to place a photograph of your dog on the reward poster. If you don't have a picture of your dog, you can find a photo of any breed on the Internet. Make the copy simple and direct, such as, "Please help us find Sparky, a two-year-old cocker spaniel. He was last seen in the area of [your general address]. Reward of [amount] for information leading to his return. Call [your telephone number]." If your dog is in need of any medical attention, remember to put that in bold print on the poster.

In addition to large, colorful posters, bring either your handwritten text and photo of your dog (or your computer disk with picture and text) to a copy/print shop and have them print as many leaflets as you estimate would be sufficient to hand out or place in areas where the most people live, work, or regularly commute.

Don't forget your local radio stations. Most of them make time for public service announcements during newsbreaks. Occasionally, local television news stations will provide a similar service.

Start off with a three-mile radius for the posters. Once a dog has decided to roam, for whatever reason, be aware that even a small dog may run for nearly a mile or more before it stops. A big, strong dog may run five miles before it stops to survey the new territory.

Another reason for the importance of haste is the likelihood that your dog will have tried to find its way back home after it exhausted itself in the mad dash to escape boredom. A problem arises when the reality sets in that it wasn't really paying attention to its surroundings when it decided to explore new territory. Self-confidence fades when the once adventurous dog finds itself among unfamiliar surroundings, unfamiliar smells, and new obstacles, such as heavy traffic, unfriendly dogs, and, sometimes a hostile environment.

If after three days you don't have your dog back home, take your posters to a fifty-mile radius. Dogs have been known to travel a hundred miles from their homes within three days. Some people will give up after a couple of weeks, but remember that people have found their dogs a year or even years later.

Stay as positive as you can. On an average, most dogs that have strayed are found within a two-mile radius of their homes. If you have a gregarious dog, it will most likely be seeking hospitable humans after its run has left it thirsty and hungry. If you have kept your pet's tags up to date, someone will quickly make the deduction that the hungry, thirsty, friendly dog has an owner who is going frantic looking for it. If your dog is shy or distrusting of strangers, it is likely to seek a safe hiding place, but hunger and thirst will eventually bring it to the attention of humans in the area.

If you have not received that most welcome telephone call reporting that someone has found your dog, it might well be time to go beyond posters and leaflets. Go to the Yellow Pages in your telephone book and mail a letter-size poster to veterinarians, kennels, dog groomers, animal hospitals, and pet stores. Why pet stores? Remember a previous chapter that warned about the menace of dognappers.

The Internet has also proven to be a marvelous new tool in helping owners retrieve their missing dogs. Many pet shelters and animal-rescue groups are online with their own Web sites. In addition, Facebook has become another new source of friends who will help you search for your dog.

FACEBOOK FRIENDS HELPED CHAZ COME HOME

On July 1, 2011, Susie Klimkiewicz of Waterford Township, Michigan, received a call from her brother, who was in an ambulance after his car rolled over on Grand Blanc Road near US 23. He told her that he had suffered only minor cuts and bruises but that his girlfriend had been critically injured. They were on their way to the hospital, he said, but he was concerned about Chaz, his mixed-breed dog, who had been riding with them as they drove up north to celebrate the Fourth of July weekend.

Klimkiewicz told Nyssa Rabinowitz of the *Flint Journal* (July 7, 2011) that while she drove immediately to the site of the car crash, she found no trace of Chaz. She did locate witnesses to the accident who stated that they had seen a dog fly out of the vehicle, land on all fours, and take off running.

When Klimkiewicz shared the account of the missing Chaz with friends and family, they created "The Champions of Chaz" on the "Reuniting Lost Dog with Owners" page on Facebook. Within a few days, Chaz had more than 425 fans.

When Michelle Guswiller saw the posting on Facebook the day of the accident, she created a flyer with Chaz's picture and description and distributed them around the area of the crash site. On July 7, a resident on Torrey Road returned home from a July Fourth holiday to find his mailbox stuffed. Among the pieces of mail, he found Guswiller's flyer about the missing Chaz. It only took one quick look from him to realize that he had seen the dog nearby.

Guswiller told the *Flint Journal* that upon receiving the man's call, she "just drove there and picked Chaz up." She said that she was very happy to be a part of the emotional reunion with Chaz and his human family.

Susie Klimkiewicz was very thankful for the help that the family received from the Facebook group, stating that she was not certain that they would have found Chaz without such prompt and generous aid. Chaz's veterinarian report indicated no injuries apart from a small fracture on his hip.

THE MIRACLE OF MICROCHIPS

If your dog is often left alone in the yard because of your family's schedule and you feel there is a chance that he or she might be tempted to roam or wander in search of new adventures to break the boredom, you might consider placing a microchip in your pet.

Microchipping involves your veterinarian implanting a minute, rice-grain-size chip under your dog's skin. It is painless, and it will enable your dog to be identified with a scanner. A great advantage of the microchip is that even if your dog loses its collar with its identification tags, it can still be identified by a veterinarian or animal shelter and be brought home to you.

A Microchip Brought Pooh Bear Home After Six Years

In 1996, lively, energetic Poquito Oso Negro, a six-pound Pomeranian ball of fluff also known as Pooh Bear, disappeared from the backyard of her home in Panama City, Florida. Her owner, Bambi Lesne, was devastated. Pooh went everywhere with her. Pooh was like one of her own human children.

Lesne was heartbroken. She had owned Pooh Bear for seven years, and they had developed a love and an intimacy that was now suddenly shattered. They had so many special little rituals that they would perform together. And now both of their lives had been torn apart by cruel circumstances or by a heartless thief who had broken into the Lesne backyard and stolen Pooh Bear.

Lesne did everything she could possibly think of to regain her beloved Pomeranian. She offered rewards on posters that she plastered throughout Panama City. She searched the side streets and byways of the city until she had completely exhausted herself and every possible avenue that could reclaim her Pooh Bear.

It was not until July 5, 2002, that a woman who wants only to be known as Peggy found a wretched, filthy, bedraggled stray Pomeranian roaming the streets of Cincinnati, Ohio, 620 miles north of Panama City, Florida. Peggy took the dirty little dog home, gave her a good bath, and had her checked by a veterinarian.

As Dr. Cheryl Devine of the Oak Crest Animal Hospital was examining the little Pomeranian, who she noted was quite old, she discovered a microchip between its shoulder blades. Dr. Devine was quite excited by this discovery, because the injection of microchips into pets had not become popular in the United States until around 2001. It was rare to find one in a dog of this age.

Because of the microchip, a joyous but somewhat overwhelmed Bambi Lesne received a call from Cincinnati, informing her that her beloved Pooh Bear, who had been missing for six years, had been found. On July 17, 2002, the Good Samaritan Peggy flew to Florida with Pooh to be certain that the little dog made it safely to her owner's arms after so many unknown adventures.

When Lesne at last held her beloved Pooh Bear in her arms once again, she saw that the thirteen-year-old Pomeranian now sported a gray muzzle, but she appeared healthy — and very happy to be back home in the warm climate of Panama City rather than trying to stay alive on the cold, wintery streets of Cincinnati.

Tom Quimby of the *News Herald* (July 14, 2008) reported that Bambi Lesne said that the return of Pooh Bear proved to her that miracles do happen. A miracle, her veterinarian might add, that could not have come to fruition without the help of a kind stranger and a tiny microchip between the Pomeranian's shoulder blades.

COOPER CAME HOME FROM THREE THOUSAND MILES AWAY AND TWO YEARS MISSING

Cooper, a small Chihuahua, disappeared from his home in California in September 2009. Almost exactly two years to the day, Cooper was found wandering the streets of Brandon, Florida, a location nearly three thousand miles away from where he was last seen by his owners. A local animal hospital found the Home-Again microchip in Cooper's body and notified his owners, who were delighted to learn that he was alive and well. How he got to Florida is anyone's guess. The grim specter of a dognapper seems likely, though Cooper may also have been picked up by someone from Florida visiting California who thought the Chihuahua was a homeless stray.

PARKER, MISSING FOR SIX YEARS, FOUND ONLY ONE HUNDRED MILES AWAY

One day in 2005, John Ollberding of Alexandria, Kentucky, let Parker, the family's shih tzu, outside to do his "business." Later, when Ollberding opened the door to let Parker back in the house, the dog was nowhere to be seen. Parker was just one year old at the time and he had always come right back in when he was called, so Ollberding thought that the pup would not have gone far. After he loaded the kids up and they drove around calling for Parker, the family just knew that something was very wrong.

The years passed. The Ollberdings moved to Melbourne, Kentucky, and in 2009 finally decided to get a new dog. A few months later, they got another.

On February 16, 2011, Michael Moore of the Humane Society of Indianapolis, Indiana, found an embedded microchip in a shih tzu that had been dropped off by a jogger, who saw a dog with matted fur, but seemingly well-fed and cared for. The jogger felt that the dog had gone missing and someone would be looking for it. What he couldn't have guessed was that a family had given up looking for the shih tzu years ago.

Moore contacted the Ollberdings, who

had a difficult time believing that Parker, missing for six years, had been found one hundred miles away in Indiana. On February 18, they made the drive from Melbourne, Kentucky, to Indianapolis to reclaim that long-missing pet that had been found. John Ollberding told reporter Keesha Richardson that ten dollars for the microchipping service was surely money well spent.

DOGNAPPED CANE FOUND FIVE YEARS LATER JUST FIVE MILES FROM HOME

Just before Christmas in 2006, someone dognapped Cane, a white boxer, from Kendra Claridy and Kayla Burton's front yard in Lakeland, Florida. After an extensive search, the owners reluctantly gave up hope of ever seeing their beloved dog again. But five years later, in August 2011, the Polk County Sheriff's Office Animal Control Shelter called to give them the wonderful news that a woman had found Cane about five miles from where he had gone missing five years ago. The information on Cane's microchip was still valid, so the happy owners were able to pick him up at the shelter and enjoy a wonderful reunion, made all the more poignant because their other dog had died two weeks previously.

SANTA'S ELVES BUSY RETURNING DOGNAPPED DOGS TO THEIR OWNERS

In December 2011, Santa's elves were busy seeing to it that missing dogs — some of them for as long as five years — were returned to their owners. That is, Santa's elves armed with microchips.

Leo

It was violation enough of the sanctity of one's home when burglars ransacked the home of a Ft. Lauderdale woman on December 23, 2011, but the thieves added the cruelty of taking her Yorkshire terrier, Leo. Anita MacLannan wasted no time in hiring a pet detective and his K9 four-legged assistant to sniff out the burglars' scent and to recover Leo. The television set and her jewelry could be replaced, but not her Yorkie. A Miami Beach Police officer spotted Leo wandering on the beach on Christmas Eve, and MacLannan got her baby Leo back in time for Christmas.

Taz

In 2006, Taz and Tyson, two Chihuahuas owned by the Magnussen family of Central Valley, California, got out of the yard of the home that the Magnussens were renting while they were building a new house. They found Tyson wandering the neighborhood, but Taz was nowhere to be seen or recovered.

On December 23, 2011, Taz was spotted, dirty and disheveled, in the parking lot of the Berkeley Bowl by a produce clerk, who turned him over to a couple, the McMullens, who were longtime customers and who also owned a Chihuahua. Although Taz got along well with their pet, named Clarence after the angel who got his wings in *It's a Wonderful Life,* the McMullens intuitively knew that someone somewhere was missing this little guy that had a mouth that appeared to form a sweet smile. Within a few hours, the McMullens took Taz to the Berkeley Animal Care Service, who located the microchip and called the Magnussens. Within hours, Taz was given a warm Christmas welcome by the family who had lost him five years before. He appeared to be in good health, and he immediately responded to the name "Taz." He immediately recognized the Magnussens and their daughters, who had been eleven and thirteen when he had gone missing, as well as Tyson, now eleven, and he unhesitatingly warmed to Zoey, a two-year-old Chihuahua.

DOGNAPPED IN FLORIDA, MIKAYLA IS REUNITED WITH FAMILY IN TENNESSEE TWO YEARS LATER

In 2009, when Charlie and Alison Murphy lived in Tampa, Florida, someone dognapped their white husky, Mikayla. The culprit had gone to great lengths to steal the dog from the Murphys' yard, breaking into her kennel, cutting the lock on her cage and slicing off her collar. Upon discovering that Mikayla was missing, the Murphys felt a great sense of loss. Wondering why anyone would do such a horrible thing, they compared stealing a family's dog to taking a family's child.

Devastated at their loss, the Murphys spent every spare moment for six months driving countless miles before they gave up the search. In addition, their friends often joined in the hunt and remained on the alert for a stray husky on the streets or by the side of the road. The Murphy family had had Mikayla microchipped, and they hoped that the procedure might prove to be as valuable in recovering their stolen dog as they had been led to believe.

Sometime after losing their beloved Mikayla, the Murphys moved to Layfatte, Tennessee. On November 30, 2011, two years after their husky had been dognapped in Tampa, they received an astonishing telephone call from the Macon County Hospital. A man had found Mikayla, thin and undernourished, there in Tennessee. He had taken her home with him and kept her for six weeks, restoring her health. Shortly after the dog had regained her strength, he had a dream in which he was shown that Mikayla might have a chip in her skin that would identify her and her rightful owners.

Todd Dunn of WKRN-TV in Nashville reported that the dream prompted the Good Samaritan to take Mikayla to a veterinarian, who indeed found and read the chip under her skin and began the search that eventually located the Murphys right there in the same state.

The Murphys had had no reason to update the data on Mikayla's chip following their move to Tennessee — assuming that she was lost to them forever — but the staff was able to locate them because the veterinarians had the necessary information on the family's other pet.

How the dognapped husky got to Tennessee is anyone's guess. Perhaps by an extraordinary coincidence the dognapper who had taken Mikayla in Florida may have moved to Tennessee sometime in that same two-year period when the Murphy family moved.

Or had Mikayla managed to escape from her captor in Florida and set out to find the Murphys in a place where she had never been, guided only by the powerful dog-human bond and the mysterious canine sixth sense? In either instance, we believe that it was another true four-legged miracle.

AFTERWORD

You've seen many times in this book how the dog-human bond and the remarkable love the two species have for each other have been the forces behind these Four-Legged Miracles. In account after account, dogs demonstrate their unstoppable drive to return to their owners at any distance or at the cost of any suffering or sacrifice.

Brian Hare, a Harvard psychologist, agrees that such a bond exists and notes that dogs are marvelously skilled at reading human patterns of social behavior. Our dogs are adept at determining our moods and what makes us happy. They are also gifted in knowing when we are sad and need someone to listen to our troubles. No other creature on Earth desires to please its human family as does the dog.

As we stated earlier, humans and dogs evolved together throughout the centuries, intensifying the bond between them. We, the authors, believe that we as a society are undergoing an exponential leap in consciousness that acknowledges the intelligence of dogs. This new awareness is leading to a deeper understanding between humans and dogs, and to canines' ever-expanding, irreplaceable roles in our society as integral helpers. In many instances, they possess talents that surpass those of humans. As we have witnessed in the stories in this book, dogs' seemingly supernatural ability to find their way home translates easily to their ability to find missing persons. Their super senses are also capable of sniffing out diseases, warning of impending seizures, and detecting dangerous explosives and harmful chemicals. Their heightened sense of empathy enables them to become the perfect therapists in hospitals, in homes for the elderly, and in private homes as companions and guides for the physically handicapped. No creature on the planet is a greater teacher of unconditional love than our dogs.

ABOUT THE AUTHOR

BRAD STEIGER and **SHERRY HANSEN STEIGER** have — together and separately — written more than one hundred books including *Christmas Miracles* (winner of the 2002 Storytelling Award from *Storytelling World* magazine) and *Dog Miracles.* The Steigers have appeared on *Hard Copy, Inside Edition,* and *Entertainment Tonight,* and in specials on HBO, Discovery, History, and A&E. They were featured in twenty-two episodes of the syndicated series *Could It Be a Miracle?*

The employees of Thorndike Press hope you have enjoyed this Large Print book. All our Thorndike, Wheeler, and Kennebec Large Print titles are designed for easy reading, and all our books are made to last. Other Thorndike Press Large Print books are available at your library, through selected bookstores, or directly from us.

For information about titles, please call:
  (800) 223-1244

or visit our Web site at:
  http://gale.cengage.com/thorndike

To share your comments, please write:
  Publisher
  Thorndike Press
  10 Water St., Suite 310
  Waterville, ME 04901